Contents

Contents

Cure Your Phobia in 24 Hours

Richard Reid

Vermilion

LONDON

1 3 5 7 9 10 8 6 4 2

Vermilion, an imprint of Ebury Publishing,
20 Vauxhall Bridge Road,
London SW1V 2SA

Vermilion is part of the Penguin Random House group of companies
whose addresses can be found at global.penguinrandomhouse.com

Penguin
Random House
UK

First published in the United Kingdom by Vermilion in 2017

www.penguin.co.uk

A CIP catalogue record for this book is available from the British Library

ISBN 9781785041297

Typeset in India by Integra Software Services Pvt. Ltd, Pondicherry

Printed and bound in Great Britain by Clays Ltd, St Ives PLC

Penguin Random House is committed to a sustainable future for
our business, our readers and our planet. This book is made from
Forest Stewardship Council® certified paper.

Introduction

You've got a phobia. This is no ordinary fear, but one that's got 'out of proportion', meaning it's controlling you, rather than you controlling it. There are things you stop yourself from doing in case you come across whatever it is that makes you scared; maybe you've changed jobs or houses, or lost touch with friends because of it. It could be affecting your relationship with your family, even with your children.

You're wondering if there's any way of dealing with it. Will you have to live with your phobia for ever? Would it be possible to wake up each morning, knowing there's nothing you have to avoid or make excuses for? What would it be like to live without this extreme fear?

Can this book cure my phobia?

That's an understandable question, and the answer is: it most certainly can.

In this book, I'll give you a step by step system to getting over your phobia … in **less than 24 hours**.

Yes – just 24 hours' commitment from you, spaced out over the course of a matter of days or weeks, is all that you need to be free of your phobia once and for all.

In the first part I explain the reasons why you have your phobia and how your brain tricks you into thinking you need to be scared, when you don't. In the second part I give you a simple process for gradually exposing yourself to what you're afraid of in an ultra-manageable way, at the end of which you'll no longer have your phobia. And in the third part I cement your new 'phobia-free' self so it never comes back. There's even a chapter for your friends and family to read as well.

As a professional and qualified therapist I've worked with countless phobia sufferers over the years, and with each one I've been able to get them from feeling terrified to being able to cope with their fear, provided they were committed to the process. The case studies and success stories in this book are there for a reason:

to convince you that no phobia is too deep-rooted to shift. Even yours.

Now I want to spread the word more widely, so everyone with a phobia can learn to live free from extreme fear.

Can a book really help me on its own?

You might be feeling a bit sceptical, wondering if a book on its own can give you such a fundamental transformation. The simple answer is: yes, it can. But as well as using this book as a standalone tool, you can also read it alongside other support. This could consist of close and trusted friends or family, or a professional therapist.

If you're keen to seek professional help, there are around 4,000 different approaches to therapy, making it difficult to know where to start. After reading this book, you'll have a good idea about what kind is best for you, so you can find someone who offers a similar style.

I've helped many, many people just like you to overcome their phobia so I know what works and what doesn't. Those people were terrified of birds, deep water, heights, or certain foods, to name a few. Some of them had suffered for decades. Now they're able to go about their lives without worrying they'll not be able to cope with the day-to-day activities most people take for granted, and the increase in their confidence levels is wonderful.

You see, I know what makes you feel irrationally scared, and I also know how to help you take that fear away. The good news is that you already have the tools within you to understand and gradually overcome your phobia so you emerge at the end phobia-free.

My process is not a magic solution and it does involve you stepping outside your comfort zone. But this is a very practical, hands-on guide: in fact, you could call it a handbook to beating your phobia. I'll be with you at every step of the way.

Having a phobia isn't as unusual as you might think

How many people know about your phobia? I'm guessing not many; I know from talking to my clients they often feel ashamed and embarrassed about what scares them. So it stands to reason that other people may also be hiding their phobias from you.

There are countless phobias in this world, and many of them have their own name. Some of them you'll have heard of, such as agoraphobia and claustrophobia. Others you won't, such as agliophobia (fear of pain), hylophobia (fear of forests), and rupophobia (fear of dirt). The point is, these names wouldn't exist if many people all over the world, since time began, hadn't been suffering just like you are.

Having a phobia doesn't mean you can't be successful in life. Many of my clients with phobias feel a failure, and assume it's somehow indicative of the kind of person they are. Nothing could be further from the truth: it's an *aspect* of who they are, not the whole picture.

Many celebrities also have phobias, and whether you're a celebrity-watcher or not this list proves there are people who manage to excel in their own fields despite their fears. Here are some examples:

Gustave Eiffel, the designer of the Eiffel Tower, was terrified of heights.

Matthew McConaughey, the Hollywood actor, is scared of revolving doors.

Johnny Depp has a phobia of clowns. *'There's something about the painted face, the fake smile. There always seems to be a darkness lurking under the surface, a potential for real evil.'*

Nicole Kidman is afraid of butterflies. As a young girl, she wouldn't even enter her home if a butterfly was sitting on the entrance gate.

Billy Bob Thornton is scared of antique furniture.

Alfred Hitchcock was terrified of eggs.

Walt Disney was, ironically, scared of mice.

These are popular legends and may not all bear the closest scrutiny, but they do illustrate how people we admire can also be affected by phobias. You're in good company.

Why you need to start now

I want to take you back to when you were a child. What did the seven-year-old you dream of becoming? In your teenage years, what job and lifestyle did you aspire to have?

Now I'd like you to consider the extent to which your phobia gets in the way of you being that person you hoped to be. Think about it not only in terms of feeling too scared to do some of the things you wanted to do, but also about the damage it does to your confidence. The problem with having a phobia for a long time is that it can feel normal. Let the realisation of how it's restricting your life be the wake-up call you need. You're letting that seven-year-old down by staying in your comfort zone and not moving on.

And what about your family and loved ones? Your partner may be at the end of their tether, wondering how they're going to cope with the adaptations they're constantly having to make, or you may be concerned you're passing your fears on to your children.

One of my clients moved house twenty-seven times in five years because of his spider phobia. Another took her university degree online due to her terror of birds; she was worried she might come across one at the train station. They're both phobia-free now, having decided they didn't want their lives to be crippled by fear any longer.

This is the best bit

I've saved this until last. Getting rid of your phobia doesn't only mean you're free to live your life without it – it gets much better than that. The very process of overcoming your deepest, darkest fear gives you the knowledge you can change almost anything for the better. Once you've had the courage to take on the challenges I'll be setting you, you'll be ready for anything. Most people will never have this experience; you could consider yourself fortunate you have the chance.

This is why I wrote this book: so you could beat your phobia, and in doing so, learn to create the life you truly want. Start reading it right now, so you can give yourself the gift of as many phobia-free years as possible. I'm looking forward to working with you.

About me

I'm Richard Reid. At this point, you might want to know a bit about me, and what makes me qualified to help you with your phobia.

I've been working as a psychotherapist and counsellor for over ten years now, and I'm a trauma and psychological resilience expert. I help my clients with a whole range of personal issues, from serious mental illnesses through to improving a certain aspect of their lives, such as confidence or sporting performance. I've even helped people who were involved in some very high-profile incidents, such as the 7 July bombings in London.

The driving force behind what I do is to make psychotherapy accessible to as many people as possible. Unfortunately, a lot of people think psychotherapy isn't for them, or that needing it makes a bad statement about the kind of person they are. Nothing could be further from the truth.

For most of my professional career, I've had a special interest in working with people with phobias. I've always been fascinated by the way in which some people who, while seemingly very capable and rational on the outside, can become paralysed by irrational fears on the inside. Some of the situations that these people find frightening, such as exposure to snakes or heights, can seem understandable to others. But it seems less obvious when it comes to being terrified of buttons, baked beans or rubber.

In my work, I've dealt with all these phobias and many more. One of my greatest satisfactions is being able to resolve some very 'niche' phobias in a matter of minutes, such as the time I cured a woman of her fear of bananas simply by showing her how to replace the negative feeling with a positive one. This process is called 'anchoring' (but more on that later in this book!).

Other clients of mine have had more complex phobias. One woman had an intense fear of signing her name in public; it took her several weeks to get over her phobia and I needed to employ a much more painstaking methodology for her situation. But the good news is that in every phobia case, provided that my client had a commitment to the process, I have been able to achieve a positive outcome **within less than 24 hours** of effort.

As part of my mission to make treatment for phobias more accessible to all, I have been a resident expert on the Sky 1 TV series *Extreme Phobias, Extreme Cures.* In this programme, I work with a number of phobia sufferers to help them to deal with their challenge. By taking them from being paralysed by their fears to being well on the way to living a normal life, I show our viewers that overcoming a phobia is completely possible.

Although a lot of my work is with private individuals, I also use my professional expertise in organisations such as the City of London Police, Ernst & Young and Morgan Stanley, to name but a few.

You can find out more about what I do via my website: http://www.RichardReidMedia.com

My story

Okay, so I'm a psychotherapist, but first and foremost I'm also a human being (you'll be relieved to know!). Most people would probably regard me as being very confident and assertive. However, it hasn't always been the case.

Until my mid-twenties I struggled pretty badly with anxiety, especially in social environments and public-speaking situations. If you asked the people who knew me at that time, they probably wouldn't have guessed I was so anxious as I was very good at hiding it. I covered up my anxiety using a combination of avoidance, bravado, humour and alcohol. Ultimately, none of these approaches resolved the underlying problem. They simply suppressed it and reinforced the belief that I was incapable of dealing with my issue without the aid of props or artificial stimulants. I was also deeply ashamed of my situation, which meant that I was reluctant to talk to anyone about it or to seek out professional help.

I'll let you into another secret ... For many years, I also contended with a deep-seated phobia of being in the sea. I have a couple of theories about what may have caused this. Firstly, neither of my parents have ever been particularly confident about being in the sea, so presumably I would have picked up non-verbal cues from their behaviours which shaped my own beliefs. However, the main catalyst for me seems to have been watching the film *Jaws* as a child and being absolutely petrified. I clearly remember jumping out my skin at the point where the skinny-dipping girl gets pulled under the water at the start of the film. For years, I would actively avoid going above waist deep in the water. I can even remember one time on a lads' holiday in Ibiza when someone proposed a swimming race at sea. Peer pressure dictated that I felt obliged to take part, but I can assure you that you have never seen anyone swim as fast as I did that day!

Even though I didn't necessarily realise it at the time, in both examples above, I eventually overcame my long-term fear permanently by retraining my brain. In a nutshell, this took the form of repeated and increasingly challenging exposure to my fears, coupled with some handy cognitive restructuring courtesy of *Meditations* by the philosopher-emperor, Marcus Aurelius (I was studying Latin and Ancient Greek at university at the time). There were bumps and setbacks along the way and it required courage and perseverance, but the hard work eventually paid off.

I now teach a fast-track version of these same skills to others in my work as a therapist and coach. I also gain regular employment as a motivational speaker, and now actively embrace public-speaking. You will also be pleased to know that I am now a seasoned scuba diver (I even came face-to-face with a shark on a night dive off the Great Barrier Reef and it was nowhere near as bad as I imagined!).

Part 1

Getting Ready to Lose Your Phobia

Chapter 1

Why Have I Got a Phobia?

O ne of the questions my clients often ask me is, 'How did I get this phobia? Why me?'

It's natural to want to know the answer, because getting an understanding of why phobias exist and how some people come to have one, is a great way to start moving past the fear. So this chapter explains the professional thinking behind phobias and why they arise.

Phobias protect us

I'm going to tell you something you'll not have thought of before. Having a phobia is actually the result of your brain doing what it's *meant to do*.

Yes, really. How come?

320 million years ago, humans and reptiles were closely related. We humans even share 98 per cent of our genes with our closest animal relative, the chimpanzee. We've done a good job of evolving since those early years, of course, but genetically speaking we've been the same for the last 200,000 years.

So what does this have to do with phobias? Well, our brains are made up of three different parts:

- **The reptilian brain:** This is the most primitive part of our brain, dealing with instinctive responses to stimuli such as pain or shock.
- **The mammalian brain:** This is slightly more advanced and is where our emotions, such as anger, fear and anxiety come from.
- **The frontal cortex:** This is unique to humans and is where we do all our rational thinking and process our speech.

As you can see, although we live in a modern world, some areas of our brain still work in a prehistoric way. And when we see a situation as threatening, the way our brain protects us is to switch immediately to the more primitive part, bypassing our frontal cortex and leaving our rational judgement out of the picture. After all, if a lion is about to attack you, don't want to ponder on what you should do, do you? You need to get out of danger straightaway.

To use a couple of stereotypes, think of your reptilian brain as being like the school bully, and your frontal cortex as being like the wimpy geek in class. When you're in danger, your bully brain leaps into action, overpowering your geek brain so it never gets a chance to think things through.

This can lead us to associate certain events with fear. So if we once had a frightening experience with a bird, for instance, and this gets imprinted on our brain, it doesn't matter how much we *tell ourselves* that not all birds are out to attack us, our ability to think rationally gets thrown out of the window by our bully brain as soon as we see it, because our frontal cortex (or our geek brain) was never involved in the first place.

This all starts to make more sense later in this book when I explain how important it is to placate that reptilian part of your brain. You need to do this before using more rational approaches, because if you don't deal with the primitive brain first, you won't get past the first hurdle.

At the moment, hopefully it's just helpful for you to know that having a phobia doesn't mean there is anything 'wrong' with you – it's just your brain protecting you from danger as it's being doing since the beginning of time.

The amygdala and our fear response

While we're talking about how our brains work, it's also worth understanding a bit more about how they deal with fear.

I expect you've heard of the 'fight or flight' response. It's when we experience a sudden threat and our body switches into survival mode – we either fight off our attacker, flee the scene or can't decide between the two and freeze. We know we're in this state because we break out into a sweat, our hearts race and our breathing gets faster.

So what does our amygdala have to do with this? Well, it's the fear sensor in our heads and it's part of (you guessed it) the reptilian part of our brain. It's our amygdala that's responsible for triggering our automatic fear response before we've even had a chance to decide whether or not a situation is dangerous.

As I mentioned before, this is very helpful for us in genuinely dangerous circumstances, but becomes a problem when it's repeated in non-life-threatening scenarios.

I want you to know about this, because being in a prolonged state of fear creates anxiety, and anxiety is all about speed and immediate reactions. So later on in this book when I teach you ways of slowing your reactions down, that's the reason.

Why else do we have phobias?

We've seen that the evolution of our brains is a contributing factor towards us having phobias. But what else is at play? There are various other things to consider:

- **Cultural factors:** Certain things are more scary in some cultures than others. For example, in some Asian countries dogs are seen as a threat, and not as cuddly pets like they are in the West. For this reason, I tend to find that Asian people are more likely to have dog phobias than other cultural groups.
- **Historical factors:** In years gone by, when we lived in closer contact with nature, there would have been a very good reason to avoid potentially dangerous animals such as snakes. This seems to have become embedded within our brains. To illustrate this,

research has shown that when monkeys are raised in captivity they can still show a fear response when they see a picture of a snake – even though they've never been exposed to one in real life.

- **Vulnerable circumstances:** Some phobias can arise during periods of particular vulnerability, such as in pregnancy, illness or extreme stress. If you think about it, it makes sense that our brains would try to protect us from any danger during this time, and if this tendency gets out of control it can develop into a phobia. One example (which is more common than you might think) is of someone getting on a crowded commuter train with a bad hangover, having a panic attack due to feeling ill, and then developing a phobia of being on trains.

- **Traumatic situations:** This is how many phobias start. A small child is asleep in their buggy while their mother pushes them around the supermarket. She goes to get an item of food off the shelf, at which point the child wakes up and panics because there's nobody there. As their mum returns, the first thing they see is the tin of baked beans she's carrying, and they associate their fear with that object. This is called 'anchoring' and we'll be covering it later in this book.

- **Social factors:**
  - **Films and the media.** *How many open water phobias have been triggered by the film* Jaws? *Even though we know very few people get attacked by sharks, that film has heightened our sense of risk about being in the water. This was certainly the case for me; I developed a fear of open water through watching that movie as a child, but through qualifying as a scuba diver I've learned that it's the thought of coming into contact with sharks, and not the reality, that's scary. In addition, in some movies certain animals are used as motifs – think of spiders and snakes in the* Raiders of the Lost Ark *series, for instance.*
  - **Colours.** *Although it's not very common, if someone has a colour phobia it is usually of the colour yellow. Many animals, and some people, are also wary of the colours yellow and black (the symbol for poison is often a black skull on a yellow background).*

What all these factors have in common is that they illustrate how our primitive brain is paying more attention to these situations than they really 'deserve'.

Why me?

'Okay,' you're saying to yourself, 'I can see why phobias might happen. But no one else I know has a phobia and they've have similar experiences to me. So why have I got a phobia and not them?'

First of all, as I mentioned during the Introduction, having a phobia is more common than you probably think. Even if we don't all have actual phobias, each one of us has got a deep-seated fear of something. Another thing to consider is that for many people their phobias are kept safely under lock and key because they are easy to avoid; it's only when they have a fear of something which is part of everyday life that it becomes a stumbling block. That's when they tend to call it a phobia.

But having said that, you're right – some people have phobias and some do not. No psychotherapist has all the answers for this, although we can identify some likely reasons:

- **A specific traumatic experience.** For instance, I went on a radio show to talk about phobias and it turned out the presenter had a phobia of escalators. The root of this had been a few years earlier when he saw a child have a bad accident on one. Our brains make generalisations: they don't always discriminate between rational and irrational fears.

- **Our family.** Some people with phobias have grown up in a family in which there were a lot of fears and anxieties. While working on the TV show *Extreme Phobias, Extreme Cures* I found that – especially with fears of dogs, birds and spiders – the people we helped tended to have siblings or parents with that same phobia. For many of them, one of the things that drove them to take part in the programme was that they were starting to notice their children were showing the same fears. So why are families so important here?

  - *We take our lead from our parents. It stands to reason that, if an adult who was influential in your life is scared of something, then you might be as well.*

  - *Of course, as a parent the last thing we want to do is to pass on our phobia to our kids, but even when we try desperately hard not to show our fear we will naturally steer away from situations which would expose us to them. That means our children never get the chance to feel comfortable with those situations.*

- *Anxiety is closely linked to phobias (I'll go into more detail about this later in this book). If we grew up in an 'anxious family' we might have instinctively created rules which made us feel safer. Some of these rules can involve avoiding certain things or situations, which can lead to developing a phobia about them.*

One final thing

If you're like most phobics, the origins of your fear are based in your early childhood and are outside of your memory. So while it's helpful to understand why phobias arise, please don't spend a lot of time trying to pinpoint the reason for yours. If this book helps you to identify it, then that could be helpful, but it's more likely you'll never know the reason behind it.

I don't want you to become stuck at the stage of asking, 'Why?' You are where you are. If you're beating yourself up looking for the root cause of your fear, then you're putting your energy in the wrong place.

It's what you *do* about your phobia *now* that matters, not what caused it all those years ago.

What we learned in Chapter 1

- Most people have either a phobia or a deep-seated fear of something – it's more normal than you might think.

- Our brains have not fully evolved to allow us to discriminate between rational and irrational fears – in essence, a phobia is a way of keeping ourselves safe.

- Apart from the way in which our brains work, there are various other causes of phobias:
  - *Cultural factors*
  - *Historical factors*
  - *Being in vulnerable or traumatic situations*
  - *Social factors*

- There are also various reasons why some people suffer from phobias and others do not:
  - *Some people have phobias that are easier to ignore (so in their own minds they're not a phobic)*
  - *A specific traumatic experience*
  - *Family factors*

- You will probably never learn the root cause of your phobia, so please don't put your energy into this. Focus instead on how you're going to get rid of your fear.

Chapter 2

What Can I Do About My Phobia?

In my professional practice I've never worked with a client who couldn't overcome their fear, as long as they had the right mindset and approach. So the good news is, as long as you have a commitment to the process, it's completely possible for you to cure your phobia in less than 24 hours. In this chapter you'll learn the basic principles for doing just that.

Helping yourself gradually

I need to be honest with you: there is no easy, pain-free way to overcome your phobia. This means that in order for you to beat your fear, you're going to need to expose yourself gradually to the very thing you're afraid of.

Now before you close this book and move on, let me reassure you I'll be helping you every step of the way. This entire book is geared towards you working on your fear *gradually*. There are no nasty shocks, sudden exposures or 'in at the deep end' philosophies here. You may have heard of a technique called 'flooding', in which phobics are immersed in a frightening situation; unsurprisingly, this creates a huge level of anxiety and can set people back unless it's done with close professional support.

Instead I'll be pacing your progress and teaching you the very same techniques I use with my private clients. When I work with a client one-to-one, it goes like this:

1. We start off by exploring their phobia and the impact it's having on their life.
2. We agree a plan of action.
3. After a couple of sessions in which I teach them how to manage their fear response, we go out into the world (either with me accompanying them, or on their own).
4. We tweak the process as we go along.

5. After a series of gradual exposures to the source of their fear, my clients are able to tolerate more and more, until they are finally free of their phobia.

And this is exactly the approach I'm taking in this book, because I know it works.

My clients never fail, because every setback is viewed as *feedback* not failure. If problems arise, we talk about what they learned and how they'd do it differently next time. The only hard-and-fast rules I set are that we keep moving forwards and talking positively to ourselves.

If you think about it, you've done this before. Whenever we learn anything new, it takes us outside of our comfort zone. Think back to when you learned to drive; you'll remember how nervous you felt when you first got behind the wheel, but because you really really wanted to do it you stuck at it. Now you're an experienced driver, I bet it doesn't occur to you to feel nervous when you get in your car – in fact, you probably chat to your driving companion and change channels on the radio while you're going along. And how has this happened? Only through gradual and repetitive exposure to the act of driving.

Getting 'used' to being in the presence of what you fear is no different.

Staying power

You know when you go to the seaside and you think about going for a swim? Brrrr! You dip your toes in, feel the icy chill and run straight back out. It's a shock to the system, isn't it?

It's like this when you're trying to confront your phobia – it's *normal* to feel uncomfortable when you put yourself out there. You feel like running away.

But what would happen if instead of jumping straight out, you were to wade out into the water and then – taking a deep breath – dip your head under? You would get an initial shudder of discomfort, for sure. But if you stayed where you were, you would start to get used to the temperature. Overcoming a phobia is very much like this – you're going to feel uncomfortable at the start, but if you carry on getting used to it, it will feel okay.

Therapists call this the 'window of tolerance'. Everybody (even you) has level of discomfort that you can deal with. The trick is to gradually edge outside of your comfort zone so your window is opened wider and wider.

If you don't think you can do this, trust me when I say you can: the success stories throughout this book prove it. Even if you're worried about having a panic attack, I'll help you through that process. While it's normal to feel a crescendo of anxiety when you're in a scary situation, it will ease if you give it time. Even if you have a panic attack, remember that nobody has ever died from one.

The truth is you need to be prepared to make yourself feel uncomfortable when you're on this journey of overcoming your phobia. But you'll be doing it gradually so it's at a pace you can cope with.

Keeping positive

I've talked about moving towards your fears gradually, and keeping going when it gets tough. But just as important is keeping a positive mental attitude.

One of the things I hear a lot from my clients is, 'I can't do this; I'm never going to get through it; I'm so useless', and so on. This is a negative thinking pattern, and it won't help you at all.

You will have setbacks, and you will find the journey hard. But for every problem you encounter, guess what? It's not a failure, it's a success.

How come? Because for everything that doesn't go the way you want it to, you will learn something. If you have a panic attack but manage to stay in your phobia situation and not run away, you'll not have failed because you had a panic attack. On the contrary, you'll have learned that if you stay with your fear, the panicky feelings will gradually subside and you'll be okay. Think about what you have achieved, rather than what you have not.

Make me a promise. As you go through this book and take action to overcome your phobia, every time you don't get quite as far as you would like, recite to yourself, 'I've achieved something even by putting myself in this situation. What can I praise myself for?' Even reading this far in the book is a step in the right direction.

If you're feeling panicked, you can think of any negative thoughts as an old friend you've grown away from – someone who's trying to hold you back to make themselves feel more comfortable. It's not your own voice you're hearing, it's just a thought that happened to come up; it doesn't mean it's true or that you have to listen to it.

Talking about how friends can either help or hinder you brings me on to buddies, which I'll explain next.

How to choose your buddy

Having a buddy is really important in helping you to overcome your phobia. You're going to be stretching your boundaries to a point where you'll be needing strong emotional support, and people who have a trusted partner in the process generally do better than those who don't.

It's a bit like having a personal trainer at the gym. You could go on your own and you'd probably improve to certain extent. Or you could have somebody by your side, encouraging you that little bit further each time so you reach your goal more quickly and reliably. That's how your buddy can help.

So who could be your buddy? They could be a trusted family member or friend, as trust is certainly important. Consider the characteristics of the ideal buddy before you decide.

A good buddy will:

- Be supportive and kind, but also won't let you get away with things
- Help you tweak your progress as you go along
- Keep you accountable
- Give you ongoing support and encouragement
- Be firm but empathetic

When you're thinking about who could help, please bear in mind that often our loved ones – through a desire to protect us – help to shield us from difficult situations. This actually makes things worse for us, because then it's so much easier for us to avoid the things we're scared of.

For instance, there was someone I worked with who was afraid of dogs, and when she went out she would get her daughter and sister to walk either side of her so she didn't have to look at any dogs she came across. Out of love and concern for her, they engineered everything around helping her to avoid her phobia. So in her situation they might not have been the best people to help her get over it.

Have you thought about teaming up with someone else with a phobia? While filming the TV show *Extreme*

Phobias, Extreme Cures, in which I helped groups of phobia sufferers to overcome their fears, the group members gave each other tremendous support. Being with each other helped to normalise the experience for them, and of course their special insight meant that they could empathise with one other very well.

Plus, as so often happens when you put people together, the group dynamics kicked in and enabled people to go much further than they would have done on their own. How often have you done something because you didn't want to lose face, or because you were thinking about other people's needs instead of your own? These factors can help you to move above and beyond your fear, and do things you wouldn't think you'd be capable of.

You probably won't be able to find a whole group of fellow phobics, but teaming up with even one would be a help.

Professional help

If you feel you would like the help of a qualified therapist, there are a number of different approaches available to you. There are many, many different therapeutic approaches to phobia treatment, and choosing which one is right for you can be overwhelming. To help you narrow it down I'm giving you my preferred options here:

- **EMDR:** (Eye Movement Desensitisation and Reprocessing). This sounds unusual, but is a great treatment if your phobia is attached to a particular event or if you know its origins.
- **Hypnotherapy:** This helps you to relax and is good for either unlocking and addressing the root causes of your phobia, or for helping you to gradually become desensitised to the fear through visualisation techniques.
- **CBT:** (Cognitive Behavioural Therapy). This is where you see a therapist who will help you learn techniques for managing your fears more effectively; after that you go out on your own to put the exercises into practice. Some CBT therapists, especially those who specialise in phobias, will come out and do them with you.
- **Exposure Therapy:** I particularly recommend this one, and it's also the treatment this book is based on.

The main point is that there is professional help out there if you need it. So if you feel after reading this book that you really don't want to go it alone, then these are some good options. But don't feel that it's only one or the other; I'd encourage you to try the techniques in this book first, with the professional support as a fall-back if you need it.

There is a list of approved associations for therapists in the Support Materials section at the end of this book. I recommend you use it as a starting point, as unfortunately there is no legal requirement for therapists to qualify before they start practising. By choosing someone who has volunteered to be regulated you are much more likely to get a professional standard of care.

What we learned in Chapter 2

- Overcoming your phobia will involve gradually exposing yourself to what you're afraid of.
- I will be helping you with this every step of the way.
- Through gradual exposure you will eventually beat your fear, but only if you stick at it.
- There is no failure, only feedback.
- Choosing a buddy to help is a great way to feel supported yet challenged.
- There is professional help out there if you need it.

Chapter 3

Panic Attacks

Learning how to cope with panic attacks is a fundamental part of overcoming your phobia. If you're like many phobics, you'll have experienced one at some point; if you're not sure if you've actually had an attack, here's what it feels like:

- You feel overwhelmed by racing, irrational thoughts (maybe you think you're going mad).
- You have a tightness in your chest (you might think you're having a heart attack).
- Your breathing is difficult.
- You're hyperventilating (breathing too quickly).
- You might have an 'out of body' experience where you feel like you're floating above yourself.
- You might faint.
- You can go pale and withdrawn.

What is a panic attack?

So what is a panic attack?

It's a state of heightened anxiety. Sometimes when people have one, they either think they're going mad or having a heart attack. As a result, it's not uncommon for them to end up in hospital before they realise what it actually is.

If you've not read Chapter 1, this is a good time to go back and review it, as many of the things I explain there about how our brains react to fear are relevant to how we deal with panic attacks.

What causes them?

They can come about for a number of reasons, either because of particular events or due to a build-up of anxiety and stress over time. Here are some examples of the causes of panic attacks:

- A specific, stressful situation. This doesn't necessarily have to be the classic example of a job interview or an exam, it can be something as everyday as getting on to a commuter train on your way to work. It's an unnatural environment, people are squashed together, you go through dark tunnels, and you're probably not feeling your best first thing in the morning.

- A prolonged period of stress or anxiety. In this case, a panic attack is your body shouting at you to listen to it, so you address the underlying problem.

- Too much boozy drinking. Alcohol is a depressant and can trigger low moods. A classic example is that of a person who goes on a drinking holiday and, due to the combination of alcohol and an unfamiliar environment, has a panic attack.

What these examples have in common is that the body's fear response (which I explained in Chapter 1) has been activated because it thinks you are in danger. Of course, you're not really in any danger – you're just on a commuter train or on holiday – but the primitive, 'fear response' part of your brain doesn't realise this.

What do panic attacks have to do with my phobia?

Panic attacks are associated with phobias in two ways:

1. They can arise when someone with a phobia is exposed to the thing they fear.

2. They can be a cause of a phobia. Using the train example above, if someone has a panic attack on a crowded train, they can associate their underlying anxiety with being on the train. This then becomes the focus for their phobia.

To make matters worse, as I'm sure you know if you've suffered from panic attacks, even thinking about your phobia or about having an attack can induce one in itself. Then it starts to become a self-fulfilling prophesy, as this creates anxiety, which in turn can trigger – you guessed it – a panic attack.

How do I deal with my panic attacks?

Being susceptible to panic attacks can be embarrassing and it's easy to feel stigmatised; the last thing you want is for people to find out you have this 'weakness', so you tend to sweep it under the carpet. That's understandable, but it only makes things worse, as a panic attack is *trying to get you to take notice of what's wrong*. If you tell it to shut up, this can intensify the experience. Imagine your panic attack as being like a two-year-old child: you ask it to keep quiet so you can have some peace, but when did a toddler ever listen to a reasonable request? Instead, he starts screaming and throwing things, and the more you yell at him to stop, the worse it gets. It just doesn't work.

'Okay,' you're saying, 'I know there's no point in ignoring or covering up my panic attacks, but what do I do instead?'

There are a series of approaches that you can take. I'll list them here so you can see them at a glance, and then I'll go into more detail on each one:

- Acceptance
- Coping strategies when you're having an attack
  - *Preparation*
  - *Staying in the present moment*
  - *Breathing exercises*
  - *Positive affirmations*
  - *Diet, lifestyle and attitude changes*

Try to accept your panic attacks

Yes, you read that correctly! The more you fight your attacks, the more power you give them. If you're like most people you're so caught up with thinking, 'I mustn't have a panic attack' that it fuels your anxiety, which in turn makes it more likely you'll go on to have one. If you can acknowledge and accept your attacks they will happen far less frequently.

So if you're going into a potential 'trigger' situation (that is, a situation in which you are likely to come across the object of your phobia), the best approach is to accept that if a panic attack happens, it happens.

This is incredibly hard, but think about it like this instead. Have you ever built up a disaster scenario in your head like this one? 'I'm going to have a panic attack, and all these people are going to see it, and then I might faint and fall in front of the train', and so on. This is called catastrophising, or imagining the worst-case scenario even though it's very unlikely to happen. In the cold light of day, I'm sure you can see how over the top this thinking is, but as your anxiety increases, the primitive part of your brain has difficulty distinguishing between real and imagined thought. So if you create a picture in your mind of something terrible happening, you will experience some of the physical sensations that go with it before it even happens. This in turn will make you more anxious and prone to having an attack.

Coping strategies for when you're having an attack

'Okay,' you're thinking, 'I know I need to be more accepting of my panic attacks, but what do I do when I'm actually having one?' This is a good question and I've laid out some techniques for you below.

Stay in the present moment

Staying in the present moment (which is also known as mindfulness) not only helps you to let thoughts come and go without getting caught up in them, but it also promotes the ability to let your feelings be as they are without trying to control them.

When, as I described above, you leap ahead in your imagination to what will happen if you have an attack, it's like adding another layer of anxiety. Then if you start avoiding the situations that make you anxious, you add another level, and so on.

So a great way of dealing with an attack as it happens is to focus on what's going on around you *right now*. Diverting your attention away from yourself and your panicky feelings, and outwards towards your environment, will not only distract you from the horrible sensations inside but will also get you back to reality.

Notice the floor or the ground you're standing on, be aware of the immediate objects around you, focus on the people you are with and how they might be feeling. Even thinking something like, 'Oh, there's a man with a briefcase, he must be going to work, I wonder what he does?' will have the magical effect of taking you out of your panicked state and into a more normal experience.

There are other exercises to encourage your thoughts to be more grounded, which I've included below.

STAYING IN THE PRESENT: EXERCISES

Even five minutes' practice a day can make a substantial difference over a period of time. It's not always easier, as it's not how the brain likes to work, so don't be surprised or put-off if you find it difficult (or even infuriating!) to begin with. In fact, the harder that you find it, the more important that it is to keep going!

Here are six short mindfulness exercises you should be able to incorporate into your daily routine without too much disruption:

1. *Two mindful bites*
   For the first two bites of any meal or snack that you eat, pay attention to the sensory experiences – the texture, taste, smell, and appearance of the food – and the sounds when you bite into your food.

   You do not need to savour per se, you are just paying attention to your sensory experience in an experiential rather than evaluative way.

2. *What one breath feels like*
   Pay attention to what one breath feels like.

   Feel the sensations of one breath flowing into and out from your body. Notice the sensations in your nostrils, your shoulders, your ribcage, your belly etc.

3. *Take a mindful moment to give your brain a break instead of checking your email*
Instead of checking your email every five minutes, spend a few seconds noticing your surroundings, for example, watching the leaves fluttering on the trees out the window.

   Use mindfulness to give your brain a break rather than filling up every tiny space in your day by automatically reaching to check your email.

4. *Air on exposed skin*
Pay attention to the feeling of air on your skin for 10–60 seconds. This is best done with some skin exposed.

5. *Scan your body*
Scan your body from head to toe for any sensations of discomfort or tension. Attempt to soften to the sensations of discomfort. Next, scan your body for any sensations of comfort or ease.

6. *Do one action mindfully*
Pick an action you do at the same time every day and plan to do that action mindfully. For example, the moment you flick out your rolled-up newspaper, or taking a bite of a sandwich and noticing the texture in your mouth.

Breathing exercises

There's a particular kind of breathing that's very helpful when you're experiencing a panic attack, as it convinces your mind and body that everything is okay. It's called 4–4–6.

Here's how it works. Breathe in for the count of 4, hold your breath for 4, and breathe out for 6. If you do this for a period of time, it regulates your breathing, starts to reduce your panic attack, and gives you something else to focus on. If you are genuinely concentrating on your breathing, you can't be consumed with anxious thoughts.

EARTH, AIR, WATER, FIRE

This is a powerful exercise that combines mindfulness – staying in the present moment – with the 4–4–6 breathing method. Take time to practise this exercise and use it whenever you start feeling anxious.

Earth

- Sit in a chair with your feet firmly touching the ground.

- Spend a few moments slowly scanning your body, noticing where your body contacts the chair and with the ground.

- Slowly scan your immediate environment and focus on two or three objects in turn and study them in detail as if you have never noticed them before.

Air

- Breathe slowly and regularly noticing the physical sensations of the act of breathing

- Breathe out for slightly longer than you breathe in (4–4–6)

Water

- Create some saliva in your mouth or suck on a boiled sweet.

Fire

- Think of a situation when you felt really calm and image that you are back there now. Notice what tells you that you are calm in that situation by engaging all your senses.

- Alternatively, try to think of a scene (e.g. a lake, beach, mountainside), a person or a metaphor that you associate with calmness or strength.

Positive affirmations

These are positive phrases you can say to yourself, which calm you down and help you to feel more in control. Following is a list of suggested affirmations, and many people find them incredibly helpful. Pick two or three that work for you.

POSITIVE AFFIRMATIONS: EXERCISES

One method for dealing with anxiety is the use of positive affirmations. When said either out loud or in our head they can positively influence our focus and remind us that there is another way of approaching the situation.

Here are a few suggestions that you may like to try:

- Even though I feel anxious, I will get through this.

- My *anxiety* is bad, but *I'm* not bad.

- I don't always *have* to feel comfortable, and it isn't awful when I don't.

- It is not necessary to be in perfect control of my anxious moments. To demand that I be in control only multiplies my symptoms.

- Others are not required to treat me with kid gloves when I feel uncomfortable.

- The world doesn't have to make it easy for me to get a handle on my anxiety.

- Anxiety is a part of life; it is not *bigger* than life.

- I can take my anxiety with me when going places and doing things that I am reluctant to do (or stay isolated).

- Controlling my anxiety is important, but hardly urgent.

- Comfort is nice, but not necessary.

- I don't have to hassle myself or put myself down for not coping better with my anxiety.

- This will pass.

- I can blend in with the flow of my anxiety; I don't have to go tooth-and-nail, head-on with it.

- If I feel anxious, I feel anxious – tough!

- I may *have* my anxiety, but I am *not* my anxiety.

Diet, lifestyle and attitude changes

This might surprise you, but you can reduce your chances of having a panic attack considerably by paying attention to what you eat and drink and how you live your life. I know you're probably more interested in learning how to cope with an attack than in putting preventative measures in place, but some of the tips I'm giving you here might even stop your attacks altogether.

Caffeine

When I worked at Transport for London I treated a guy who had panic attacks and anxiety. To be honest, I was really scratching my head to find out what might be causing his problem. Towards the end of the session I asked him, almost out of desperation, what he ate and drank. He said, 'I have a few cups of tea at work.'

I replied, 'How many cups of tea?'

'Twenty a day.'

That's a lot of caffeine! I advised him to cut out the tea and come back in two weeks, at which point his anxiety had gone.

This is an extreme example, but it just goes to show how much caffeine can play a part. The reason we perk up with caffeine is that our body is working under stress because it thinks it's being poisoned. And as we know, anything associated with stress is a potential cause of a panic attack.

Alcohol

I've already mentioned how alcohol is a depressant and can contribute to anxiety and panic attacks. What's more, if you've got a hangover you're bound to be at a lower ebb, which can itself trigger an attack. It's worth monitoring your panic attacks to see if they are related to alcohol consumption in some way.

Recreational drugs

It's not uncommon for people who take recreational drugs to have panic attacks. Cannabis especially can make you feel anxious and paranoid, so even if you feel you get a short term feel-good effect from drugs, in the long term they are counterproductive.

Stress

When you worry a lot about things, these thoughts can generate physical responses in your body, gradually building up to panic attacks. Work, lack of sleep, and unresolved issues such as grief or emotional stress can also play their part.

To counter this, it's a great idea to become more body-aware. We tend to go through life being constantly busy, which means we don't have the time or inclination to check in with ourselves as to what's happening in our body and our emotions. If we acknowledge what's going on while it's happening, these residual worries are less likely to build up and come out in a bad way. Something as simple as pausing and checking in with yourself once an hour, can help to pre-empt a panic attack.

Mindfulness, which I touched on briefly on page 53, is a huge topic which deserves a book of its own. But please take a look at the Monkey Mind exercise below; it's a very simple and effective system which will help you to become more calm and body aware.

MONKEY MIND

Imagine that you can compare your mind with the activities of a monkey. Whenever it wants to go anywhere, it goes from tree to tree, often getting distracted by bits of fruit or other animals.

It starts off with the goal in mind but gets easily distracted by a hundred things. Our minds are very like this. We start with a thought and very soon our mind takes us to the past or the future and away from our focus.

It is difficult to get a monkey to do what you want it to do and likewise it is difficult to get the mind to focus on one thing at a time.

With this in mind, try the following exercise:

- Start by getting comfortable and bringing your attention inwards

- Just follow your breath and relax

- As you start to breathe, begin to count 1 for an in and an out breath

- Keep counting up to 21, one count for each in and out breath

- Stay focused without trying too hard

- Every time you find your mind thinking about other things, start again at 1, just leading it back patiently

- Start to practice this for a few minutes at first. You might be surprised how often you lose count!

- Keep patient and persevere. This is a very effective exercise for training the mind.

Be prepared

Once you've decided what techniques are best for you, you need to plan ahead. The midst of an attack is not the best time to try out new techniques; for a start, you're unlikely to even remember them, and secondly you're not in the right frame of mind to put them to use as a beginner.

Regular practice creates shortcuts in your brain which help you to get around your stress response (which is what an anxiety attack is). One of the things I learned in my work with the City of London Police, is that all the emergency services rehearse things time and again, so when they're in a real life crisis the habit kicks in automatically. This is what you can do too.

So how do you 'practise' having a panic attack so you can rehearse your coping strategies? It's a three step process:

1. Go over your coping techniques repeatedly.
2. Think about your trigger situation or a time when you've had an attack, and allow yourself to start feeling the anxiety. Just imagine it.
3. Practise using the techniques while feeling anxious, and see how they bring your stress levels down.

This will have two effects: it will prove to you that the techniques work, and it will help you to put them into practice in a real event. What's more, just the reassurance that you know what to do and how to cope will mean you're less likely to have an attack in the first place.

It won't last for ever

Finally, when you're in the middle of a panic attack it's really important to remind yourself that anxiety is a short-term thing and will pass. Your body can't keep up a state of heightened fear for ever, and you know this because you've never had an attack that lasted permanently, right?

The reality is that panic attacks happen to you and you need to find a way to deal with them, rather than demanding they don't happen. This means being accepting of yourself, and even forgiving yourself for having these episodes. Every time you learn to deal with them you're a step closer to overcoming them. It's human nature to want to remove yourself from uncomfortable situations, but unfortunately with panic attacks that doesn't work, so you need to learn how to manage them as a 'friend'.

One of the best ways to do this is through positive, rather than negative, self-talk. Read the next chapter to find out more about that.

What we learned in Chapter Three

- A panic attack is a state of heightened anxiety, which can feel both physically and emotionally overwhelming
- Panic attacks can be caused by short or long term triggers, and these underlying causes need to be addressed in order for the attacks to stop.
- They're connected to phobias because they can be caused by being in a frightening situation, and also because they can sometimes lead to phobias in their own right.
- To deal with your panic attacks:
  - *Try to accept them*
  - *Focus on the present moment*
  - *Do breathing exercises*
  - *Say positive affirmations*
  - *Have a healthy diet and lifestyle*
  - *Deal with unresolved stress in your life*
  - *Practise coping strategies ahead of time*
  - *Remember they're only short term*

Chapter 4

Self-Talk

As a therapist it's relatively easy for me to spot the things my phobia clients are doing that hold them back. It's a bit more difficult for them to do this for themselves. The best example of this is negative self-talk, so in this chapter you'll learn why the way you talk to yourself matters, and what you can do about it.

People with phobias tend to focus on what they *didn't* do rather than what they *did* do; this came out very strongly when I was working on the TV Series *Extreme Phobias, Extreme Cures*. The participants gave themselves an incredibly hard time, saying things like, 'I'm so stupid; everyone else can do this; what's wrong with me?' and so on.

Does this ring a bell for you? If it doesn't, it might be because you've grown so accustomed to your negative internal voice that you don't notice it any more.

Maybe you even assume everyone talks to themselves in this way.

You don't have be like this – it really is optional. Just think: are the things you say to yourself the things you'd say to a good friend? If they were having a hard time dealing with their fears, would you be as unsupportive and unhelpful to them as you are being to yourself? I'm sure you wouldn't be.

What has negative self-talk got to do with my phobia?

A negative thought is a defensive thought; it's based on the assumption you're under some kind of threat. And if you keep having these thoughts, your brain gets tricked into believing something terrible is going to happen. This in itself can trigger a panic attack or some other kind of negative mood, which is incredibly unhelpful when you're trying to overcome your phobia.

Also, talking to yourself in a negative way makes you feel like you can't deal with your problems. After all, someone who is useless and stupid couldn't possibly beat a phobia, could they? But you know from reading this book you *can* do this, so your put-down comments are the opposite of what's really true.

The 10 types of negative self-talk

As I mentioned before, negative self-talk can be so habitual you don't even realise you're doing it. So I'm giving you a list of the top 10 types – many of which I'm sure you'll start to recognise:

1. **All-or-nothing thinking:** You look at things in a 'black-and-white' way. If something goes badly it's a disaster, never a minor problem.

2. **Over-generalisation:** If something goes wrong you see it as part of a pattern of defeat, rather than as a one-off incident. Finding yourself saying something 'always' or 'never' happens is a sign that you're over-generalising.

3. **Mental filter:** You ignore the positives and focus on the negatives.

4. **Discounting the positives:** You insist your achievements and positive qualities 'don't count'; only your shortcomings are worth focusing on.

5. **Jumping to conclusions. (A) Mind-reading:** You assume people are reacting negatively to you when

there's no evidence for it (B) **Fortune-telling:** You predict things will go wrong without any good reason for it.

6. **Magnification or minimisation:** You blow bad things out of proportion or shrink the importance of good things.

7. **Emotional reasoning:** You create logic from how you feel: 'I *feel* like an idiot, so I must be one.'

8. **'Should' statements:** You criticise yourself by saying 'should', 'shouldn't', 'must', 'ought', and 'have to'.

9. **Labelling:** You identify with your shortcomings. Instead of saying, 'I made a mistake,' you tell yourself, 'I'm a loser'.

10. **Personalisation and blame:** You blame yourself for something you weren't completely responsible for, or you blame other people and overlook how you might have contributed to the situation.

If you thought you weren't a negative self-talker before, hopefully you've become more aware of it by now. And by the way, *everyone* does this to some extent, not just you. The reason I'm addressing this issue now, is because how you talk to yourself as a phobia sufferer makes a massive difference to how quickly you can overcome your fear. The more positive your words, the better your progress will be.

Okay, I admit it: I'm a negative self-talker. What do I do now?

Because we tend not to realise we're having these negative thoughts, we assume they're the reality of the situation. Retraining our brains to think positively on a *day-to-day* basis, means that when a difficult situation arises we're more likely to talk to ourselves constructively than critically – and eventually do it automatically.

Day-to-day

First of all, try to catch yourself when you're engaging in negative self-talk; you might find it's only in hindsight you realise what you were doing, but simply being aware is the first step. By the way, once you become aware, it goes without saying that you see this as feedback not failure – don't make things worse by criticising yourself for being negative!

Then, see if you can turn the talk around in a positive way. An everyday example of how you talk to yourself might go something like this:

'Why did I forget the car keys again? I'm such an idiot.'

To turn this around positively, you could change it to:

'Aargh, I forgot the car keys again, how annoying. Oh well, at least I remembered the shopping today. And no one's perfect.'

Can you see how much better you would feel after the positive switch-around? If you were this person, your fear and stress levels would be lower, your attitude more 'can do' and your mind so much more accepting of change and growth. This is the kind of mentality that will help you to overcome your phobia.

In a panic attack

Once you've grown more used to talking to yourself positively every day, it will be easier to apply the same sort of thinking in a panic attack. In the last chapter, I talked about how important preparation is in dealing with panic attacks, and switching negative self-talk to positive is no different.

Here's an example of negative self-talk in the midst of a panic attack:

'There's a bird over there. I can't go near it. This always happens – I knew it would. I should never have come out today, how stupid I was to think I could cope with it.'

And the positive switch-around:

'Even though I'm having a panic attack because there's a bird over there, I'm going to be okay. I can get through this.'

You can see how acknowledging the problem is important – you're accepting it but then applying your positive intention. It's a subtle but profound shift. The words 'even though' are a really great way to get you started in your positive train of thought, because you can follow on with what the problem is (acknowledging it) and then move on to a positive alternative thought.

Feedback not failure

You'll have noticed I love the term 'feedback not failure', and it so happens it's also one of the most powerful ways of using positive self-talk. If you actively expose yourself to the source of your fear, for example, and have a panic attack, you've failed. On the contrary, you've learned something important from the experience (feedback) which you can apply next time.

For instance, if you feel anxious and panicky on a crowded train, you now have a 'thinking strategy' ready to deal with this. You're not a failure for being unable to tolerate a packed train, you've simply given yourself the opportunity to wonder why this might be. Perhaps you drank a strong coffee this morning which set you off, or you didn't get enough sleep last night.

Can you see how much more helpful this is than beating yourself up?

What we learned in Chapter Four

- Negative self-talk is really common in people with phobias.
- Criticising yourself will make it harder for you to overcome your phobia, because it puts your brain into 'fear' mode and dents your confidence.
- It's easy not to realise you're doing it, so the first step is to become more aware.
- After that, try to switch to positive versions of your negative self-talk on a day-to-day basis.
- Then, attempt to apply this during a panic attack or when you're feeling afraid.

Part 2

Losing Your Phobia

Chapter 5

Your Phobia and How to Overcome It

This is the part you're most interested in. 'Tell me – how exactly do I lose the phobia that's been dominating my life for years in less than 24 hours?'

Don't worry, in this chapter I'll explain what to do, how to do it, and ways of working through any difficulties that arise.

You may be surprised to learn that the general principles for getting over one phobia are pretty much the same as for another. However, there are also some specific differences. For that reason, I've broken down the main types of phobias into groups. If you see yours in one of the groups then you can go there, and if not simply choose the category that seems most similar to your own. Don't worry if you don't identify closely with any of the phobias in the list; as long as you follow the advice for the closest phobia to your own you will be able to overcome it step by step.

Here are the phobia categories:

- Agoraphobia (fear of open spaces and of being outside)
- Social phobia (fear of social interaction and of being with people)
- Specific phobias
  - *Animal (fear of any type of animal, bird, fish, insect or reptile)*
  - *Natural environment (fear of the natural world, such as water)*
  - *Blood injection type (fear of medical interventions including dental treatment)*
  - *Situational (fear of particular situations, such as heights)*
  - *Others (if your phobia doesn't fit into any of the above, go here)*

I'm going to turn into a bit of a school teacher now: *please, before you head off to your specific phobia section, read Chapters 1 to 4 if you haven't already.* It will make such a big difference to your progress. You can't tackle your phobia effectively until you understand how your brain works, why your support systems are important, how to deal with panic attacks, and the effects that positive and negative self-talk can have. Also, please read the rest of this introductory section below as it contains vital information for your progress.

That's the school teacher bit over with now, I promise. The rest is just solid, helpful and practical guidance.

To help you on your way, I'll be including some motivating snippets from success stories of people who have successfully overcome their phobia. They really could be you! Here's one from Louisa to get you started, in her own words:

When I was younger – about seven or eight years – I was on holiday with my parents. I went on a water slide ride. When I got to the top of the steps I noticed it was quite high and the water looked deep so I started to turn around to go back down the steps. However, this older boy pushed me down the slide and I managed to grab hold of the sides, but he fell on top of me and I went under the water. This was my trigger, the start of my phobia.

At school we used to have swimming lessons, I couldn't get in the pool. I always remember other children laughing at me. I hated it. Then as a teenager my family went on holiday and we had our own pool and villa. Gradually day by day I got in the pool with my step dad and he helped and encouraged me. However when we got home it all went back to normal. I hated swimming, and never went.

So then I was asked to appear on TV for a TV programme about phobias. Obviously mine was water. Well I tell you now I was scared, petrified at the thought of what they were going to make us do. But the things I did I've never done before.

We went out on a rigid inflatable boat – fast! I think we went 60mph! Or 50mph – can't quite remember the speed but it was quick (I loved it!) out on the sea! Me – loving the sea! Ha ha. Then we went fishing and pulled in crab baskets – out in the sea – OMG – I felt sick! Afterwards I felt so chuffed with myself. I did all of it. I DID IT!

Louisa, who had a water phobia before
she worked with me on Extreme Phobias,
Extreme Cures

How will it feel?

Prepare yourself for a bit of a roller coaster – getting over a phobia will bring you lows and highs you've never experienced before. When you're in a low, go back and read Louisa's last paragraph above, because that amazing feeling of accomplishment can be yours too. And when you're on a high, just enjoy it and feel proud of yourself.

To start off, bear in mind that we all like to stay in our comfort zone – it's natural. The thing is, though, when you're trying to overcome a phobia it's unrealistic to expect to achieve it without feeling any discomfort. You have to be prepared to go through those tricky experiences.

One of the most difficult emotions you'll come across is fear. Fear prompts us to do one of two things: remove ourselves from the situation, or rush through it so we get it over with as quickly as possible. But when you're in the process of beating your phobia, you need to do the opposite which is to *slow down*. This will feel counterintuitive and scary, because it's going against everything your mind and body are telling you to do.

What did scare me was the fear of what was planned
for us during the weekend. I was very doubtful of the
methods of treatment – I mean how could putting us
in a confined space with birds flying close to me help
when my biggest fear was being in a confined space
with birds! But somehow it did work …

Ann-Marie, who had a bird phobia before
she worked with me on Extreme Phobias,
Extreme Cures.

This is not an 'all-or-nothing' process. It's about
feeling some of the fear but not traumatising yourself
by going too far, too fast. A *slow build-up* is best, and
repetition of your experience is also vital. As you start
to master your anxiety, you're educating the primitive
part of your brain to believe there really is nothing to
fear.

I walked across a bridge over a barge; I jumped
into a very deep filled tank of water and it was
freezing; I floated with a life jacket on! I had a
moment when I cried. I thought about giving up.
No one was holding me there or telling me I had to
do any of it. I think I had to hit the 'wall' so to
speak and have that moment to realise I'm human.

I have limits and I have to climb over the 'wall' and get on with the task in hand. So I got out and jumped back in that tank of deep water and I was so proud of myself. I cried again but this time it was happy tears!

Louisa

Every single person I've ever worked with on their phobia has felt just like you are now, and the same as Ann-Marie and Louisa did at the beginning. They thought they couldn't do it, and then once they were in the situation they were tempted to believe they couldn't stay in it. But they managed it, and so can you.

So how does exposure therapy work?

Exposure therapy means putting yourself in your phobia situation in a slow, step-by-step way. Your levels start off small, and gradually get bigger and bigger as you progress. You don't move on to the next step until you feel comfortable with the one you're on, and in this way, you slowly get yourself to the point where your phobia doesn't trouble you any more. It sounds simple, and actually it is, although I don't underestimate how hard this will be for you.

The first thing you need is a clear plan of progression, which means creating an 'exposure ladder' with your first step being at the bottom and your last being at the top. See the box for how an exposure ladder is set up – there is also a template in the back of the book for you to use.

Exposure Ladder

Construct a ladder of situations that you currently avoid. At the top of the ladder put those that make you most anxious. At the bottom of the ladder put places or situations that you avoid, but which don't bother you as much. In the middle of the ladder put ones that are 'in between'. Give each item a rating from 0–100 per cent according to how anxious you would feel if you had to be in that situation. Overcome your anxiety by approaching these situations, starting from the bottom of the ladder. Repeat each stage as many times as necessary.

In each phobia group I'll give you examples of what your plan could consist of, but the steps are completely up to you. For instance, if you have a water phobia, the first step could be stepping in a puddle – or whatever contact with water causes you minimal fear. Step 10, the most difficult, could be swimming across a deep lake – or whatever activity causes you so much fear you can't even bear to think about it.

Next to each step I want you to record your anxiety level experienced when you either do the action or imagine doing it, ranked from 1 to 10, with 1 being low and 10 being high. This will help you to see how your discomfort reduces over time, which will be very motivating for you.

At the same time, I want you to record your progress after each attempt. Don't focus on what didn't go well, just make a note of it for next time and put your efforts into recording what did. Congratulate yourself as you see yourself moving forwards.

I've created a special, ready-made template ladder with anxiety and achievement recording areas, for you to download here http://richardreidmedia.com/thehub/cure_your_phobia

Activity	Anxiety Rating 0–100%	Hour 1–24	Insights & Learning
		24	
		1	

Above all else, please remember this when you create your ladder: it's not an 'all-or-nothing' scenario. Don't think, 'I've got a fear of heights, and I want to be able to go in a lift, so if I don't do that straight-away I've failed.' Throwing yourself in at the deep end will only upset you and set you back, because if it doesn't work you'll feel like you can't do it. Be kind to yourself.

How high should you go? That's up to you. One thing I can say, though, is that your highest rung on the ladder should be at least one or two steps further than you feel you really 'need' to go. For example, if you've got agoraphobia you may feel that being able to stand alone in an open field (your highest step) isn't something you really need to do, and that just being able to walk down the street is enough. This means that you *should* put standing alone in an open field, *not* walking down the street, at the top of your ladder; if you don't do this, the every-day activity that you want to accomplish without fear will always feel like a stretch to you. Does that make sense?

Dare to think outside of what you are currently capable of. You really are amazing.

Practice first

Having your ladder of progression planned out is important, but you also need to know what action to take when you hit the discomfort barrier. The first thing you'll want to do is get the hell out of the situation that's making you feel panicked, but that won't help you, so to avoid that please practise some of the techniques beforehand.

In Chapter 3 (Panic Attacks) I talked about why it's important to prepare, so if you haven't read it, then turn to it now, or review it if you have. Breathing and grounding exercises, along with practising mindfulness, are incredibly helpful here – so try them when you're in your safe zone before you get into your phobia situation.

If you don't do this, the 'fear' part of your brain may override the rational part, sending you into a tailspin.

How can I manage my anxiety? What if I get a panic attack?

First of all, practising (see the above and page 63) will help enormously, as will reviewing Chapters 1 to 4.

But you can also help yourself to feel less anxious by accepting anxiety as a normal human emotion. We tend to think about anxiety as being something terrible, and to be avoided at all costs, but actually it's just another feeling like anger, happiness or sadness.

Within each phobia group I ask you to rate your anxiety level from 1 to 10 so you can start to be less 'black and white' about it. So instead of thinking, 'I'm anxious', you can think, 'I'm feeling anxious on a level 7, but last time I tried this it was level 9, so I'm getting somewhere.' By ranking it, you get a sense of which direction it's going in, which is very motivating and helps you decide what's working and what's not. Ranking your anxiety is also a good distraction technique in itself. If you're focusing on deciding what level it's at, you're less likely to overwhelmed by the emotion.

A panic attack would be a level 10, but if you stay with the feeling it will plateau. When it eventually starts to come down, this is the moment when you're educating your brain to work more rationally. If you come out of the situation when your panic attack is at its height, all you're doing is telling your brain, 'This is dangerous, you shouldn't be doing this.' Stay there, and your brain will start to realise the anxiety is reducing, and that's when you make true progress.

How long will it take?

Here's the good news. You may be surprised to learn that during my stint on the Sky TV series *Extreme Phobias, Extreme Cures*, the phobics I worked with overcame their phobias in *three days*. Yes, really! And that was with only two hours a day of treatment and exposure therapy, so in a total of six hours each participant was able to conquer their deepest fear. I bet that sounds quicker than you expected; it certainly was for my participants. Here, I'm setting you the challenge of overcoming your phobia in less than 24 hours.

On your own it may take longer, or even less time than the TV participants, but the timescale is really up to you. Please move at your own pace, while at the same time not making the process too slow and easy for yourself – otherwise you won't get the results you're after. You need to keep up the momentum.

One thing I want to stress, though, is that once you've overcome your phobia you need to keep it going. Getting to the top rung on your ladder is fantastic, but for it to become the norm takes a bit of maintenance. The changes you're making are competing against years of phobic behaviour, so it's unrealistic to expect it all to click into place permanently after a few days. To avoid a relapse, I'd advise you to diary in some activities which take you to your top rung (or near it) on a weekly basis for the first few months, and monthly after that.

What might go wrong?

There are a number of difficulties you might come up against as you move up the ladder. They can all be overcome by re-reading Chapters 1 to 4, but I'll summarise how to deal with them here too.

I can't cope with the anxiety when I'm in my frightening situation

It's normal to feel as if you 'can't cope', but really you can. Practise the breathing exercises you learned in Chapter 3, along with the positive self-talk in Chapter 4, and force yourself to stay in the situation. After a while, your panic will die down (it can't last for ever) and you'll learn you're capable of doing this.

There's no failure, only feedback, so after every task take some time to think about what you've learned. It might be you've discovered you need to break down the steps some more, or you could refamiliarise yourself with the calming techniques before you try again.

Talk positively to yourself. Instead of beating yourself up and saying, 'I'm so useless, everyone else can do this, why not me?' reassure yourself with, 'OKAY, I didn't manage to do it this time, but what can I learn from this experience so next time goes more smoothly? Did I forget to breathe calmly? Did I not spend enough time in the situation to allow myself to calm down? Or was I not focusing enough on things outside myself, so I allowed myself to get drowned in panic?'

There is always something to learn.

My buddy or partner gets upset when he/she sees me feeling anxious

It's natural they don't want to see you feeling frightened, especially as they may have got used to reassuring you for so long. It can be hard for them to change their approach. Refer them to Chapter 2 in which I talk about buddies, and also Chapter 8, which addresses how family and friends can help.

I've completed one step but I can't make myself move to the next one

That might be because the gap between your steps is too big. Try breaking it down into smaller chunks. For instance, you might need your buddy to stay with you at first before you go it alone, or you could find a halfway house between the two tasks that makes the transition easier.

Also, have you done each step repeatedly until it feels pretty normal? You may be moving on too quickly from one step to the next.

I've kept doing the same step over and over again but I don't feel any less anxious.

For starters, if you've managed to do the same frightening task repeatedly, you've made a massive improvement. Just by doing it, your brain is learning to cope with the situation, even if you don't consciously realise it. Congratulate yourself for getting this far, and keep going – at some point your fear will start to abate.

Also, make sure you're recording your anxiety levels accurately, as it's easy to forget how scary something was at the beginning compared with now.

Every time you confront a difficult situation, you learn more about yourself. It's a bit like peeling away the layers of an onion, as you discover more and more about your physical, emotional and mental reactions. Each set-back is just giving you more material to work with.

Now let's move on to the specific phobias.

Agoraphobia

Agoraphobia is one of the most limiting of phobias. You feel petrified at the thought of going out and about, and when you do force yourself into the 'real world' you can't wait to get back to the safety of home. This is having a cumulative effect on your freedom, your independence and your sense of 'you'.

This phobia is an irrational anxiety about being in places where escape may be difficult or embarrassing. Controlling your environment is how you've learned to deal with it, but that means you're stuck indoors while life passes you by.

You've probably also found yourself doing what we therapists call 'fortune-telling', which goes like this: 'I know I'll feel terrified as soon as I step outside, and then I'll have a panic attack'.

Although very debilitating, agoraphobia could be described as an extreme version of staying in your comfort zone. By giving into this phobia, you'll be avoiding all sorts of situations as you cocoon yourself from 'real life'. Because of this, if you have agoraphobia it's worth asking yourself the question: 'What am I trying to avoid other than just being in open spaces?' Some agoraphobics can also experience symptoms of OCD (obsessive compulsive disorder). Having some personal therapy alongside this process can be very useful, and it's something you may want to consider.

And finally, if you've dived straight into this chapter, that's understandable, but please do read Chapters 1 to 4 and the introductory section in Chapter 5 first. Absorbing these will make an enormous difference to how successful you are in beating your phobia.

Agoraphobia Exposure Ladder

First of all, create your exposure ladder. The principles of creating your ladder are:

- The bottom rung is an activity which you can do without a major problem.
- The top rung is an activity which you can (at this point in time) hardly bear to think about.
- The rungs in between (of which there can be as many or as few as you like) are the activities which gradually lead you from small discomfort to unbearable discomfort.

Sample Exposure Ladder for Agoraphobia

Construct a ladder of situations that you currently avoid. At the top of the ladder put those which make you most anxious. At the bottom of the ladder put places or situations that you avoid, but which don't bother you as much. In the middle of the ladder put ones that are 'in between'. Give each item a rating from 0–100% according to how anxious you would feel if you had to be in that situation. Overcome your anxiety by approaching these situations, starting from the bottom of the ladder. Repeat each stage as many times as necessary.

Here's my example ladder to get you started, but yours can be completely different. Please don't feel

Activity	Anxiety Rating 0–100%	Hour 1–24	Insights & Learning
On your own, go into a wide-open space for half an hour			
With your buddy, go into a wide-open space for half an hour			
On your own, go into your local town centre for half an hour			
With your buddy, go into your local town centre for half an hour			
On your own, go to a local shop for 15 minutes			
With your buddy, go to a local shop for 15 minutes			
On your own, go to the end of your street			
With your buddy, go to the end of your street			
Step outside your front door for 10 minutes			
Look out of the window in your home for 5 minutes (whatever view feels safest to you)			

embarrassed by any of the items on the ladder – they are for your eyes only (and that of your buddy too, ideally).

I've created a special, ready-made template ladder with anxiety and achievement recording areas, for you to download here http://richardreidmedia.com/thehub/cure_your_phobia

Next to each rung, put a date for when you are going to try the activity, and beside that record your level of discomfort when doing it, marked from 1 to 10. You'll need to do each activity *several times* before you move on to the harder one, so your brain has time to learn you're not in danger when you do it. The experience should feel pretty normal before you move on.

When you're setting your timescales, be realistic but not *too* easy on yourself. Consider what you want to achieve and by when, so you're maintaining a continual sense of moving forward. However, don't be afraid to revise the timescales if you find the steps are too big!

You'll see there are time limits for the activities and this is important. Making yourself stay in the situation for a pre-arranged period of time is fundamental to your progress, because you need to allow your brain to catch up with the idea that you can do this. If you panic and shorten it don't worry, just try again another time; but always aim to achieve your time target in the end.

After each step, take some time to reflect on what happened during your encounter. Being as objective as you can, ask yourself: did the world out there do you any harm, or were you able to come home safely?

Only move on to the next rung of the ladder once you feel comfortable with where you are now. If you hit a barrier don't worry, just try again another day. Also check out 'What might go wrong?' in the first section of Chapter 5 (see page 91).

Social Phobias

If you have a social phobia you'll find interacting with other people very frightening. Maybe you get sweaty palms when you contemplate going to a party or a work meeting. Or possibly even bumping into someone in the street is enough to make you panic.

A social phobia can be extremely debilitating. It can also be confusing: you might be pretty good at interacting with people generally, but at the same time be gripped with anxiety that you're coming across in a bad way.

It's likely you're fine with small groups of people, but larger groups intimidate you to the point where you can't bear to go near them. That's because we all find it more difficult to gauge how we're perceived by larger groups, and for you that's a massive problem. Of course it could affect you the other way around, but the first way is the most common.

With a social phobia, it's very helpful for you to think about what social situations you *do* feel comfortable with. It might be when you're with your partner or family, for instance. How do you behave when you're with them? How do you breathe, relax and hold yourself? Mimicking this behaviour in a more intimidating social scenario will 'trick' your brain into thinking you feel comfortable, which in turn will make you feel as if you are. I know it will feel false to you, but to everyone around you it will just seem natural.

We therapists call this a 'pattern interrupt': just pick two or three things you do when you're at ease, and put them into action when you're not. It won't be enough to eradicate your anxiety, but it will undermine it.

Something you may have found yourself doing over the years, probably without realising it, is 'mind reading'. You make assumptions about how you come across, and what people are thinking about you, by reading their minds. Although you do this to feel safe, it's very unhelpful when you're trying to overcome a social phobia.

To get away from mind-reading, focus on the other person or people you're with, and on what's going on around you, rather than on yourself. You'll find your thoughts starting to move away from your preoccupations with your own feelings, which will be a big relief.

So to summarise:

- Work out what you do when you feel at ease with certain people, then …
- Mimic those same behaviours when you're with groups you feel anxious with
- Avoid mind reading other people by focusing on them rather than on yourself

And finally, if you've dived straight into this chapter, that's understandable, but please do read Chapters 1 to 4 and the introductory section in Chapter 5 first. Absorbing these will make an enormous difference to how successful you are in beating your phobia.

Social Phobia Exposure Ladder

First of all, create your exposure ladder. The principles of creating your ladder are:

- The bottom rung is an activity which you can do without a major problem.
- The top rung is an activity which you can (at this point in time) hardly bear to think about.
- The rungs in between (of which there can be as many or as few as you like) are the activities which gradually lead you from small discomfort to unbearable discomfort.

Sample Exposure Ladder for Social Phobias

Construct a ladder of situations that you currently avoid. At the top of the ladder put those which make you most anxious. At the bottom of the ladder put places or situations that you avoid, but which don't bother you as much. In the middle of the ladder put ones that are 'in between'. Give each item a rating from 0–100% according to how anxious you would feel if you had to be in that situation. Overcome your anxiety by approaching these situations, starting from the bottom of the ladder. Repeat each stage as many times as necessary.

Here's my example ladder to get you started, but yours can be completely different. Please don't feel embarrassed by any of the items on the ladder: they are for your eyes only (and that of your buddy too, ideally).

I've created a special, ready-made template ladder with anxiety and achievement recording areas, for you to download here http://richardreidmedia.com/thehub/cure_your_phobia

Next to each rung, put a date for when you are going to try the activity, and beside that record your level of discomfort when doing it, marked from 1 to 10. You'll need to do each activity *several times* before you move on to the harder one, so your brain has time to learn you're not in danger when you do it. The experience should feel pretty normal before you move on.

When you're setting your timescales, be realistic but not *too* easy on yourself. Consider what you want to achieve and by when, so you're maintaining a continual sense of moving forward. However, don't be afraid to revise the timescales if you find the steps are too big!

Activity	Anxiety Rating 0–100%	Hour 0–24	Insights & Learning
Give a talk or a presentation to a group of people			
On your own, approach a larger group of people you don't know and talk with them, for 10 minutes			
With your buddy, talk to a small group of people you don't know, for 20 minutes			
With your buddy, talk to a small group of acquaintances, for 20 minutes			
On your own, talk to someone you don't know in your local shop (you could ask them the time)			
With your buddy, meet up with another 2–3 friends and stay for half an hour			
On your own, go inside the pub and stay for half an hour - bring something to read if you want to			
With your buddy, go inside the pub and stay for half an hour			
On your own, go to your local pub and look in the window, imagining yourself to be inside. Stay for 5 minutes			
With your buddy, visualise going to your local pub or bar, and chatting with them			

You'll see there are time limits for the activities and this is important. Making yourself stay in the situation for a pre-arranged period of time is fundamental to your progress, because you need to allow your brain to catch up with the idea that you can do this. If you panic and shorten it don't worry, just try again another time; but always aim to achieve your time target in the end.

After each step, take some time to reflect on what happened during your encounter. Being as objective as you can, ask yourself: was there anything about the other person or people that would suggest they found you anything but normal and friendly?

Only move on to the next rung of the ladder once you feel comfortable with where you are now. If you hit a barrier don't worry, just try again another day. Also check out 'What might go wrong?' in the first section of Chapter 5 (see page 91).

Animal phobias

How embarrassing is it that you can't go to your local park because you're terrified of meeting a dog or a bird? How guilty do you feel when your kids want to go to the zoo, or when you see them starting to avoid the same animals you fear, and worry you're passing your phobia on to them? Having an animal phobia can seem so … well … ridiculous, but try telling yourself that when you're in the grip of a panic attack.

Actually, animal phobias are more common than you might think. After all, it's natural to be scared of creatures that could hurt us, like snakes and lions. In Chapter 1 there's more information on why we're more likely to be scared of some animals than others, so it's worth going back and reading that now if you haven't done so already.

I never really told people about my fears as I thought they would think I was an idiot to be afraid of something small and of what others thought of as a beautiful thing. I believed that I was the only person in the world that had this fear. I felt embarrassed and ashamed going out anywhere where there may be birds. When my daughter was young I could never take her for days out at the beach or to anywhere there may have been birds.

Ann-Marie, who had a bird phobia before she worked with me on Extreme Phobias, Extreme Cures

Unlike other phobias, animal phobias are usually (although not always) caused by a bad experience in your past.

When I was around seven years old, my friend locked me in a small bedroom with a budgie. The bird was obviously afraid and flapping around trying to get out, which frightened me as it was flying at me.

Ann-Marie

I guess I've had a dislike of birds ever since a pigeon pooped on my brand-new Goofy hat as I walked out of the Disney World gift shop. The adult I am now thinks it's daft that I let something bother me so much, but try telling the seven-year-old me that it wasn't a really big deal. I had just experienced a whole day of 'Disney Magic', and waited patiently to spend my hard-saved pocket money on the hat I'd set his heart on the moment I walked through the gates to the Magic Kingdom. Over time, my hatred of birds grew, and before I knew it I was avoiding them. Then, fast forward 20-odd years and I'm a six-foot-three-inch man

who can't even take his daughter to the local farm
because he's scared of the chickens and geese.
Guy, who had a bird phobia before he worked
with me on Extreme Phobias, Extreme Cures

So there may have been a genuine reason for you to be afraid of an animal at the time, but it's now become irrational. Or you may have a phobia of a more 'dangerous' type of creature such as snakes and spiders, but this has led you to extreme measures to avoid them. If you find yourself constantly scanning the room to check if there's a creepy-crawly lurking, you'll know what I mean.

The thing about animals is they can be unpredictable, can't they? They're not under our control. You've probably found yourself doing what we therapists call 'fortune-telling', which goes like this: 'I know that dog's going to jump at me, and then I'll have a panic attack'. This is your brain finding a way to keep control of the animal's behaviour by predicting what it will do, but all it does is make you more anxious. That's because the primitive part of your brain that processes your fear, finds it difficult to distinguish between imagination and reality. Chapter 1 explains this more fully.

Instead, try and stay grounded in the present moment. Practise your breathing exercises and focus on anything *other* than the animal itself. Instead of imagining what *might* happen, focus on what is *actually* happening around you.

And finally, if you've dived straight into this chapter, that's understandable, but please do read Chapters 1 to 4 and the introductory section in Chapter 5 first. Absorbing these will make an enormous difference to how successful you are in beating your phobia.

Animal Phobia Exposure Ladder

First of all, create your exposure ladder. The principles of creating your ladder are:

- The bottom rung is an activity which you can do without a major problem.
- The top rung is an activity which you can (at this point in time) hardly bear to think about.
- The rungs in between (of which there can be as many or as few as you like) are the activities which gradually lead you from small discomfort to unbearable discomfort.

Sample Exposure Ladder for Animal Phobias

Construct a ladder of situations that you currently avoid. At the top of the ladder put those which make you most anxious. At the bottom of the ladder put places or situations that you avoid, but which don't bother you as much. In the middle of the ladder put ones that are 'in between'. Give each item a rating from 0–100% according to how anxious you would feel if you had to be in that situation. Overcome your anxiety by approaching these situations, starting from the bottom of the ladder. Repeat each stage as many times as necessary.

Here's my example ladder to get you started, but yours can be completely different. In any case, the steps you take will be geared towards the specific animal itself. Please don't feel embarrassed by any of the items on the ladder – they are for your eyes only (and that of your buddy too, ideally).

I've created a special, ready-made template ladder with anxiety and achievement recording areas, for you to download here http://richardreidmedia.com/thehub/cure_your_phobia

Activity	Anxiety Rating 0–100%	Hour 0–24	Insights & Learning
Alone, hold the animal for 10 minutes			
With your buddy, hold the animal for 10 minutes			
Alone, touch or hold the animal briefly			
With your buddy, touch or hold the animal briefly			
Alone, approach the animal and stand beside it for ten minutes			
With your buddy, approach the animal and stand beside it for 10 minutes			
Alone, go to a place where the animal will be, keeping your distance. Do this for 20 minutes			
With your buddy, go to a place where the animal will be, keeping your distance. Do this for 20 minutes			
On your own, look at a picture of the animal for 10 minutes			
With your buddy, look at a picture of the animal for 10 minutes			

Next to each rung, put a date for when you are going to try the activity, and beside that record your level of discomfort when doing it, marked from 1 to 10. You'll need to do each activity *several times* before you move on to the harder one, so your brain has time to learn you're not in danger when you do it. The experience should feel pretty normal before you move on.

When you're setting your timescales, be realistic but not *too* easy on yourself. Consider what you want to achieve and by when, so you're maintaining a continual sense of moving forward. However, don't be afraid to revise the timescales if you find the steps are too big!

You'll see there are time limits for the activities and this is important. Making yourself stay in the situation for a pre-arranged period of time is fundamental to your progress, because you need to allow your brain to catch up with the idea that you can do this. If you panic and shorten it don't worry, just try again another time; but always aim to achieve your time target in the end.

After each step, take some time to reflect on what happened during your encounter. Being as objective as you can, ask yourself: was there anything about the animal that would suggest they were going to cause you terrible harm?

Only move on to the next rung of the ladder once you feel comfortable with where you are now. If you hit a barrier don't worry, just try again another day. Also check out 'What might go wrong?' in the first section of Chapter 5 (see page 91).

I worked hard with graded exposure which I found really helpful. Gradually building up made it more manageable on my own. ... I was absolutely terrified, and I was sure the whole time that I couldn't do it – but then I realised I'd said the same thing on every task and always managed to do it.

Kelly, who had a bird phobia until she worked with me on Extreme Phobias, Extreme Cures

Natural environment phobias

This can be a wide-ranging area. If you're wondering what natural environment phobias include, it's things like:

- Heights
- Water
- Weather
- Thunder and lightning

- The dark
- Enclosed spaces such as caves and forests
- Any other fear of the natural world around you

Being afraid of the natural elements can feel so child-ish, can't it? Surely only kids are scared of the dark, or tall trees?

Back in the days when we lived in caves it was normal to be wary of these things. Nature is so much bigger and more powerful than us, and in those days we could die of cold or be attacked by wild animals in the night. However, in our modern world we know we don't need to fear the natural world in the same way.

So you know it's irrational, but you can't stop yourself feeling terrified regardless. Maybe your phobia is of something that's avoidable most of the time, such as heights, but that means you're constantly limiting your experiences. Or it could be of something that's around you every day, such as rain or enclosed spaces.

I have a water phobia. Deep water that is, terrified of the thought of going on a boat, ferry, and I can't swim very well. I have a fear of drowning. I couldn't

put my head under the water for the fear of not
being able to lift it back up.
Louisa, who had a water phobia before she worked
with me on Extreme Phobias, Extreme Cures

The other thing about the natural world around us, is that the elements aren't under our control. We can't stop the rain falling, the sun going down, or the cliff being high. It's possible you would like your world around you to be just as you want it, and this kind of OCD (obsessive compulsive disorder) thinking is common in people who have this kind of phobia. The way you've been managing your need to control things is to avoid elements *outside* of yourself. But the way to get over your phobia is to deal with what's *inside* first. By learning to manage your internal feelings in a safe, 'practice' environment, you're training your brain to cope when you get close to the external source of your fear.

You can do this in small ways, which have nothing to do with the phobia you actually have. Think about the methods you may use to control the world around you, such as making sure your shoes are lined up in a row before you go to bed, for instance. Force yourself to stop doing that and stay with that uncomfortable feeling for a while. It will pass, and you can review Chapter 3 for further help with this.

> *I've tended to avoid situations such as tourist attractions; this has been frustrating especially with friends who I've travelled with. They feel it's illogical as it's safe and nothing is going to happen. I travelled to Paris with an ex-girlfriend and was unable to go near the Eiffel Tower as just looking at the building made me feel really sick. I'm also terrified of flying, which has caused a number of problems. When I've managed to get on a plane I'm a nervous wreck, and have to be calmed down by the airline staff.*
>
> **Peter, who had a heights phobia before he worked with me on Extreme Phobias, Extreme Cures**

Sometimes we like to kid ourselves that we have more control over things than we actually do, and it's only when something goes wrong we realise how little control we actually do have. Beating a phobia of your natural environment is all about coming to an acceptance that there's a limit to your control, and being relaxed around that idea.

Because of this, it's a good idea to avoid doing what we therapists call 'fortune-telling'. If you find yourself thinking, 'I know I'll feel terrified if it starts raining, and then I'll have a panic attack', that's when it's time to practise your calming and distraction techniques. 'Predicting' what's going to happen is simply your brain trying to control the uncontrollable.

And finally, if you've dived straight into this chapter, that's understandable, but please do read Chapters 1 to 4 and the introductory section in Chapter 5 first. Absorbing these will make an enormous difference to how successful you are in beating your phobia.

Natural Environment Phobia Exposure Ladder

First of all, create your exposure ladder. The principles of creating your ladder are:

- The bottom rung is an activity which you can do without a major problem.
- The top rung is an activity which you can (at this point in time) hardly bear to think about.

- The rungs in between (of which there can be as many or as few as you like) are the activities which gradually lead you from small discomfort to unbearable discomfort.

Sample Exposure Ladder for Natural Environment phobias

Construct a ladder of situations that you currently avoid. At the top of the ladder put those which make you most anxious. At the bottom of the ladder put places or situations that you avoid, but which don't bother you as much. In the middle of the ladder put ones that are 'in between'. Give each item a rating from 0–100% according to how anxious you would feel if you had to be in that situation. Overcome your anxiety by approaching these situations, starting from the bottom of the ladder. Repeat each stage as many times as necessary.

Here's my example ladder to get you started. Because the natural environment is so varied, I've used heights as an example, but yours might of course be a completely different phobia. Just adapt it to your own needs, and try not to be embarrassed by any of the items on the ladder – they are for your eyes only (and that of your buddy too, ideally).

Activity	Anxiety Rating 0–100%	Hour 0–24	Insights & Learning
Walk to a cliff edge or steep height and stand at the top for 20 minutes			
Alone, walk up a steep hill and look down from the top for 10 minutes			
With your buddy, walk up a steep hill and look down from the top for 10 minutes			
Alone, take an elevator in a high building and look out of the top floor window for 10 minutes.			
With your buddy, take an elevator in a high building and look out of the top floor window for 10 minutes.			
As per step 3 but from a third-storey window			
As per step 2 but from a third-storey window			
Alone, open the window and look down for 5 minutes			
With your buddy, open the window and look down for 5 minutes			
Look out of the window in the second storey of a building for 5 minutes			

I've created a special, ready-made template ladder with anxiety and achievement recording areas, for you to download here http://richardreidmedia.com/thehub/cure_your_phobia

Next to each rung, put a date for when you are going to try the activity, and beside that record your level of discomfort when doing it, marked from 1 to 10. You'll need to do each activity *several times* before you move on to the harder one, so your brain has time to learn you're not in danger when you do it. The experience should feel pretty normal before you move on.

When you're setting your timescales, be realistic but not *too* easy on yourself. Consider what you want to achieve and by when, so you're maintaining a continual sense of moving forward. However, don't be afraid to revise the timescales if you find the steps are too big!

You'll see there are time limits for the activities and this is important. Making yourself stay in the situation for a pre-arranged period of time is fundamental to your progress, because you need to allow your brain to catch up with the idea that you can do this. If you panic and shorten it don't worry, just try again another time; but always aim to achieve your time target in the end.

After each step, take some time to reflect on what happened during your encounter. Being as objective as you can, ask yourself: was there anything about the environment that suggested you were in actual danger?

Only move on to the next rung of the ladder once you feel comfortable with where you are now. If you hit a barrier don't worry, just try again another day. Also check out 'What might go wrong?' in the first section of Chapter 5 (see page 91).

I took part in Group Exposure Therapy which involved various challenges dealing with heights. I felt very uncomfortable and frightened, however the exercises proved to be beneficial ... I felt ecstatic as I conquered each challenge, however disappointed that I didn't finish the final challenge involved. I did, however, learn that I need to be kind to myself and also I learned numerous tools and techniques which helped me focus on something else as a distraction from the actual phobia and fear.

Peter

Medical phobias

Just the thought of going to the doctor, dentist or hospital makes you feel faint and anxious. Wild horses couldn't drag you to a dental check-up. And as for injections or operations, forget it.

Most people understand why you wouldn't want to go to the dentist – it's hardly everyone's favourite pastime, is it? So medical phobias aren't perhaps as embarrassing or difficult to explain as others might be. And they're not too difficult for you to avoid on a day-to-day basis.

But when you need medical attention, or find yourself avoiding routine check-ups, which are designed to prevent health problems, then it gets more serious. And constantly worrying about becoming ill, and needing the treatment you're terrified of, is draining and stressful.

What's more, if you've got a medical phobia you've probably also got some kind of untreated illness, or are storing up problems for the future by not seeking help now.

This may surprise you, but when you think about going for treatment, you quite likely turn into a 'fortune teller'. As you imagine getting to the doctor's waiting room, you're already anticipating the worst that could happen. It doesn't matter to you that thousands of people have had an injection every day and emerged unscathed, you're thinking of the one person who you know fainted on the nurse's floor. And you're convinced this time it will be you.

The Internet tends to make medical fears worse, as well. It's a breeding ground for scare stories, and encourages the idea these procedures are a lot riskier than they actually are. I'm sure you've found yourself surfing online for reassurance many times, only to find yourself feeling even more anxious than when you started.

The point I'm making is that a big part of overcoming your medical phobia is in dealing with what's *in front of you now*, rather than worrying about what *may happen in the future*. You see, it doesn't matter how much you think about what *could* happen, you're not actually going to be able to deal with it until it *does* happen (which it almost certainly won't). Does that make sense?

By accepting that you have very little control over what happens medically, ironically you're exerting the most control you can ever have. Which is the control over your own thinking.

Now you may say, 'By imagining the worst-case scenario, I'm preparing myself mentally for it. This is a good thing.' But actually, the worst almost never happens. And if it does, it's not usually the thing you've prepared for, it's something else entirely! If it's going to happen, it's going to happen, and what will equip you best to deal with it is to manage how you're feeling right now. Because if your emotions are all over the place, you're won't be able to manage a crisis.

If you think about it, it's not *you* who's going to decide whether your tooth filling goes well or badly, it's the dentist who's doing it. By constantly bracing yourself for everything to go wrong, you're heightening your anxiety which is in turn making you feel even more afraid.

Here's how to approach this phobia:

- Try to gain control over your emotional state minute by minute, focusing on the present rather than speculating about the future. 'I'm in the waiting room, I can see a child over there, there's a clock on the wall, I feel calm.'
- Leave plenty of time to get to your appointment. The adrenalin caused by being late will heighten

your anxiety. You could even walk more slowly than normal to calm yourself down. This is especially important if you tend to use delaying tactics to put off leaving the house, with the result that you're in a rush.

- While you're waiting, do some everyday things like chatting with the receptionist or reading a magazine. This will 'trick' your brain into believing that everything is okay (which of course it is).

- Be in command of the facts. Find out how many people actually die from dental treatment, or faint when they have an injection. What are the actual risks of the operation you're having?

- The more certainty you have, the more relaxed you'll feel. So ask the doctor or nurse to be explicit about what's involved in the procedure. Even if everything you hear isn't to your liking, you'll feel less anxious when you know what you're dealing with. The worry of not knowing is far worse than being in the know.

- And tell them you've got a phobia so they can help you keep calm during your treatment.

And finally, if you've dived straight into this chapter, that's understandable, but please do read Chapters

1 to 4 and the introductory section in Chapter 5 first. Absorbing these will make an enormous difference to how successful you are in beating your phobia.

Medical Phobias Exposure Ladder

First of all, create your exposure ladder. The principles of creating your ladder are:

- The bottom rung is an activity which you can do without a major problem.
- The top rung is an activity which you can (at this point in time) hardly bear to think about.
- The rungs in between (of which there can be as many or as few as you like) are the activities which gradually lead you from small discomfort to unbearable discomfort.

Sample Exposure Ladder for Medical Phobias

Construct a ladder of situations that you currently avoid. At the top of the ladder put those which make you most anxious. At the bottom of the ladder put places or situations that you avoid, but which don't bother you as much. In the middle of the ladder put ones that are 'in between'. Give each item a rating from 0–100% according to how anxious you would feel if you had to be in that situation. Overcome your anxiety by approaching these situations, starting from the bottom of the ladder. Repeat each stage as many times as necessary.

Here's my example ladder to get you started. Yours can be completely different if you like. Just adapt it to your own needs, and try not to be embarrassed by any of the items on the ladder – they are for your eyes only (and that of your buddy too, ideally).

I've created a special, ready-made template ladder with anxiety and achievement recording areas, for you to download here http://richardreidmedia.com/thehub/cure_your_phobia

Next to each rung, put a date for when you are going to try the activity, and beside that record your level of discomfort when doing it, marked from 1 to 10. You'll need to do each activity *several times* before you move on to the harder one, so your brain has time to learn you're not in danger when you do it.

Activity	Anxiety Rating 0–100%	Hour 0–24	Insights & Learning
Alone, go to a medical appointment which involves the kind of procedure you have a phobia about			
With your buddy, go to a medical appointment which involves the kind of procedure you have a phobia about.			
Alone, go to a medical appointment (it could just be a check-up)			
With your buddy, go to a medical appointment (it could just be a check-up)			
Alone, go into the medical waiting room and sit there for 20 minutes			
With your buddy, go into the medical waiting room and sit there for 20 minutes			
Alone, go to your local doctor, dentist or hospital and stand outside the door for 20 minutes			
With your buddy, go to your local doctor, dentist or hospital and stand outside the door for 20 minutes			
Watch a video of someone having a medical procedure for 10 minutes (you can find one on the Internet)			
Look at a picture of someone having a medical procedure for 10 minutes (you can find one on the Internet)			

The experience should feel pretty normal before you move on.

When you're setting your timescales, be realistic but not *too* easy on yourself. Consider what you want to achieve and by when, so you're maintaining a continual sense of moving forward. However, don't be afraid to revise the timescales if you find the steps are too big!

You'll see there are time limits for the activities and this is important. Making yourself stay in the situation for a pre-arranged period of time is fundamental to your progress, because you need to allow your brain to catch up with the idea that you can do this. If you panic and shorten it don't worry, just try again another time; but always aim to achieve your time target in the end.

After each step, take some time to reflect on what happened during your encounter. Being as objective as you can, ask yourself: was there anything about the medical experience that suggested you were in actual danger?

Only move on to the next rung of the ladder once you feel comfortable with where you are now. If you hit a barrier don't worry, just try again another day. Also check out 'What might go wrong?' in the first section of Chapter 5 (see page 91).

Situational phobias

So what's a situational phobia? Like the name suggests, it's when you have an intense fear of being in a particular situation or doing a specific thing. Here are some examples:

- Being on a train
- Enclosed spaces
- Being in a crowd
- Driving a car
- Going to the supermarket

Having a panic attack whenever you go to a restaurant, for instance, can feel downright ridiculous and embarrassing. So you avoid doing it, and the more you stay in your comfort zone by avoiding your fear, the worse the problem gets.

If you have a phobia of the London Underground, you might walk or get the bus instead. Or if you can't bear to be in a crowd, you'll go out shopping and social-ising when it's quiet. That's fine to a degree, but what happens when that friend you'd love to see can only meet up on a weekend night? Or you miss a job inter-view because your bus gets stuck in traffic and you can't bring yourself to hop on the Tube? It's so easy for your life to become limited bit by bit, until you wake up one day to the realisation your phobia is controlling and undermining your life to a level you can't live with any more.

You've probably also found yourself doing what we therapists call 'fortune-telling', which goes like this: 'I know I'll feel terrified as soon as I get in the supermar-ket, and then I'll have a panic attack'. This is the time to practise your breathing and distraction techniques, recognising this is simply your brain trying to control the uncontrollable.

In a moment we'll get on to creating your exposure ladder, but before we do that I want to make an import-ant point: preparation is key. Don't rush into each step just to get it over with, instead, take your time. If you find you feel worse when you're low on blood sugar, make sure you have something to eat before you tackle a task. Pick a time that's relatively good for you (although I understand no time is completely good right now, as you'd rather not be doing it at all), and make sure you're not pressured to be in a certain place by a certain time.

In other words, give yourself the best possible opportunity for success. Don't make this harder for yourself than it needs to be.

And finally, if you've dived straight into this chapter, that's understandable, but please do read Chapters 1 to 4 and the introductory section in Chapter 5 first. Absorbing these will make an enormous difference to how successful you are in beating your phobia.

Situational Phobias Exposure Ladder

First of all, create your exposure ladder. The principles of creating your ladder are:

- The bottom rung is an activity which you can do without a major problem.
- The top rung is an activity which you can (at this point in time) hardly bear to think about.
- The rungs in between (of which there can be as many or as few as you like) are the activities which gradually lead you from small discomfort to unbearable discomfort.

Sample Exposure Ladder for Situational Phobias

Construct a ladder of situations that you currently avoid. At the top of the ladder put those which make you most anxious. At the bottom of the ladder put places or situations that you avoid, but which don't bother you as much. In the middle of the ladder put ones that are 'in between'. Give each item a rating from 0–100% according to how anxious you would feel if you had to be in that situation. Overcome your anxiety by approaching these situations, starting from the bottom of the ladder. Repeat each stage as many times as necessary.

Here's my example ladder to get you started, using a phobia of being on a crowded train. Yours will probably look very different as situational phobias are so varied, but you can still work with the principles of the ladder. Just adapt it to your own needs, and try not to be embarrassed by any of the items on your ladder – they are for your eyes only (and that of your buddy too, ideally).

I've created a special, ready-made template ladder with anxiety and achievement recording areas, for you to download here http://richardreidmedia.com/thehub/cure_your_phobia

Activity	Anxiety Rating 0–100%	Hour 0–24	Insights & Learning
Alone and at a busy, crowded time, get on a train for a 10-minute journey with no one to meet you. Sit down if possible			
Alone at a busy, crowded time, get on a train for a 20-minute journey, but with your buddy meeting you at your destination.			
At a busy, crowded time, get on a train with your buddy for a 20-minute journey, with your buddy in a separate carriage. Stay near the door			
With your buddy and at a busier time, get on a train for a 20-minute journey. Stay near the door			
Alone and at a quiet time, get on a train for a 20-minute journey. You could arrange to meet someone at the other end			
With your buddy and at a quiet time, get on a train for a 20-minute journey			
Alone and at a busier time, go inside the entrance hall of the station and stand there for 20 minutes			
With your buddy and at a busier time, go inside the entrance hall of the station and stand there for 20 minutes			
Alone and at a quiet time, stand outside the entrance to the station for 10 minutes			
With your buddy and at a quiet time, stand outside the entrance to the station for 10 minutes			

Next to each rung, put a date for when you are going to try the activity, and beside that record your level of discomfort when doing it, marked from 1 to 10. You'll need to do each activity *several times* before you move on to the harder one, so your brain has time to learn you're not in danger when you do it. The experience should feel pretty normal before you move on.

When you're setting your timescales, be realistic but not *too* easy on yourself. Consider what you want to achieve and by when, so you're maintaining a continual sense of moving forward. However, don't be afraid to revise the timescales if you find the steps are too big!

You'll see there are time limits for the activities and this is important. Making yourself stay in the situation for a pre-arranged period of time is fundamental to your progress, because you need to allow your brain to catch up with the idea that you can do this. If you panic and shorten it don't worry, just try again another time; but always aim to achieve your time target in the end.

After each step, take some time to reflect on what happened during your encounter. Being as objective as you can, ask yourself: was there anything about the situation that suggested you were in actual danger?

Only move on to the next rung of the ladder once you feel comfortable with where you are now. If you hit a barrier don't worry, just try again another day. Also check out 'What might go wrong?' in the first section of Chapter 5 (see page 91).

Other phobias

There are so many phobias in this world. You wouldn't believe the huge variety of things that some people are mortally afraid of: buttons, baked beans, rubber, cars, parties, numbers, the moon, vomiting, knees, the number eight, signing your name in public, death, a particular country, long words, garlic, clowns, sourness, things being to your right or left, flutes, books, Halloween, the colour yellow, belly buttons, beards, falling in love, hands, chopsticks.

The list goes on. In fact, for every item or experience that exists, there will probably be at least one person who has a phobia about it.

So you can see it wouldn't be possible for me to include every single phobia in this book, but I hope by now you've gained enough insights through reading about other phobias to be able to tackle your own, whatever it is.

If your phobia doesn't fit within any of the categories so far, that's fine – we're all unique. Just use the exposure ladder example below to construct your own route out of your fear. Your specific phobia will have a hierarchy within it: for example, if you're afraid of the colour yellow, there could be different shades of yellow you find easier or more difficult to tolerate, or seeing yellow in different situations could cause varying reactions in you.

You've probably also found yourself doing what we therapists call 'fortune-telling', which goes like this: 'I know I'll feel terrified as soon as I see a clown, and then I'll have a panic attack.' This is simply your brain trying to control things by predicting the unpredictable, and once you realise that, it will be much easier to manage.

All of the steps in your ladder will involve you practising the breathing and calming strategies we've already talked about. And remember your positive self-talk and thinking! Each time you master a step on the ladder, you're getting better and better at facing your fears.

And finally, if you've dived straight into this chapter, that's understandable, but please do read Chapters 1 to 4 and the introductory section in Chapter 5 first. Absorbing these will make an enormous difference to how successful you are in beating your phobia.

Other Phobias Exposure Ladder

First of all, create your exposure ladder. The principles of creating your ladder are:

- The bottom rung is an activity which you can do without a major problem.
- The top rung is an activity which you can (at this point in time) hardly bear to think about.
- The rungs in between (of which there can be as many or as few as you like) are the activities which gradually lead you from small discomfort to unbearable discomfort.

Sample Exposure Ladder for Other Phobias

Construct a ladder of situations that you currently avoid. At the top of the ladder put those which make you most anxious. At the bottom of the ladder put places or situations that you avoid, but which don't bother you as much. In the middle of the ladder put ones that are 'in between'. Give each item a rating from 0–100% according to how anxious you would feel if you had to be in that situation. Overcome your anxiety by approaching these situations, starting from the bottom of the ladder. Repeat each stage as many times as necessary.

Here's my example ladder to get you started, using the example of a phobia of baked beans. Yours will probably look very different as phobias are so varied, but you can still work with the principles of it. Just adapt it to your own needs, and try not to be embarrassed by any of the items on your ladder – they are for your eyes only (and that of your buddy too, ideally).

I've created a special, ready-made template ladder with anxiety and achievement recording areas, for you to download here http://richardreidmedia.com/thehub/cure_your_phobia

Next to each rung, put a date for when you are going to try the activity, and beside that record your level of discomfort when doing it, marked from 1 to 10. You'll need to do each activity *several times* before you move

Activity	Anxiety Rating 0–100%	Hour 0–24	Insights & Learning
Warm up the beans, noticing how they smell, and eat a normal helping. Do this with your buddy first if you need to			
Alone, eat a spoonful of baked beans			
With your buddy, eat a spoonful of baked beans. If you must spit them out, that's fine, just try swallowing them the next time			
Alone, open the can and pour some on to a plate			
With your buddy, open the can and pour some on to a plate			
Alone, look at a can of baked beans for 10 minutes			
With your buddy, look at a real can of baked beans for 10 minutes			
Imagine pouring out some beans on to a plate			
Imagine opening the can of beans			
Look at a picture of a can of baked beans (find one online) for 10 minutes			

on to the harder one, so your brain has time to learn you're not in danger when you do it. The experience should feel pretty normal before you move on.

When you're setting your timescales, be realistic but not *too* easy on yourself. Consider what you want to achieve and by when, so you're maintaining a continual sense of moving forward. However, don't be afraid to revise the timescales if you find the steps are too big!

You'll see there are time limits for the activities and this is important. Making yourself stay in the situation for a pre-arranged period of time is fundamental to your progress, because you need to allow your brain to catch up with the idea that you can do this. If you panic and shorten it don't worry, just try again another time; but always aim to achieve your time target in the end.

After each step, take some time to reflect on what happened during your encounter. Being as objective as you can, ask yourself: was there anything about what you did that suggested you were in actual danger?

Only move on to the next rung of the ladder once you feel comfortable with where you are now. If you hit a barrier don't worry, just try again another day. Also check out 'What might go wrong?' in the first section of Chapter 5 (see page 91).

Part 3

Now You're Phobia-Free

Chapter 6

So What's Next?

This chapter is about how to live the rest of your life without your phobia. That thought feels good, doesn't it?

But first let me ask you – how did you feel when you read that first sentence? Excited, scared, horrified, or maybe even a little bit sceptical? Your answer will say a lot about how confident you are at this point in the process. Whatever your feelings are, they are completely normal, and I'll be helping you work through them as this chapter progresses.

For now, just take some time to celebrate. If you've followed the guidance in Chapter 5 and managed to get on top of your phobia, you've achieved more than most people will in their whole lives. Even if all you've done is read this book so far, you've made a mental commitment to living your life without that huge fear hanging over you.

Well done. I mean it – *really well done*.

Take a moment to think about what you're going to do to celebrate. What will you choose as a treat? Could you go out for a meal with your partner, book a spa session, meet up with a friend, or just spend a day doing something you love? If it's an activity you would never have done while you had your phobia, all the better. It's worth marking this moment, as it will give you positive thoughts to sustain you over the next few months.

There's a transition period

One of the questions my phobia clients often ask me is, 'How do I really know if I've got rid of this phobia? And what if it comes back?'

The truthful answer is, it takes time for you to prove to yourself that you've really changed. You've spent so long avoiding the thing you're afraid of it can feel awkward – wrong, even – to go about your daily life without worrying about it.

You might have expected that if you'd done the exercises everything would click into place. But actually, if you've had your phobia for 20 or 30 years, there's an adjustment period in which the reality of your achievement needs to sink in. You might still be a bit wary of going into situations which you used to be afraid of, and that's normal. You won't necessarily see the full results straight away.

Not only that, but you will now be dealing with the fact that there are things you couldn't face doing before, which you now can – and that means other activities related to them have also come into your world. For instance, if you had agoraphobia, how will you cope with going out and about, with all the expectations and challenges that brings? What will it be like to go to the supermarket or on the school run? Now, instead of hiding away at home, you'll need to keep appointments, adapt to others' lives and work with the world the same way other people have to.

Phobias often develop as a way of making us feel safe. This might sound counter-intuitive (you're probably thinking your phobia made you feel *un*safe), but actually it meant there were certain things you didn't need to confront. Now your phobia is no longer acting as a cushion between you and the world, it's time to deal with things you've been avoiding, or persuading other people to do for you. This can feel very daunting.

Of course it depends on what your phobia was. If you were terrified of something that was relatively easy to avoid, the adjustment might not be so great. But if you were scared of activities which affected your every-day life, your world has expanded enormously. Using a heights phobia as an example; now you can go on an aeroplane, up to the top of the Empire State Building, or on an escalator. Is that going to be exciting for you, or scary, or both? How will you handle it?

Slowly does it

The same principles apply for your adjustment period as were there for when you overcame your phobia in the first place. Small steps, and asking for help, are key.

Take things slowly and gradually. You might even want to create a second exposure ladder to ease you into the 'normal' world. It can be frightening to be confronted with a raft of new experiences linked to your old phobia, even if you don't have it any more. So make it easy for yourself by moving forward one step at a time.

Also, although you'll want to gradually wean your-self off your buddy, for now they're invaluable. If water was your phobia, for instance, it would be a good idea to bring them with you when you first go to the swim-ming pool. The second time they can just watch you, and the third time you can do it on your own.

Also, please don't forget your breathing and grounding techniques which you used so effectively before.

Schedule it in

It's human nature to think that once we've achieved something, we can rest on our laurels and not be so vigilant any more. Ask anyone who's lost weight only to gain it back, and you'll know exactly what I mean.

Because of this tendency we all have, it's really important to keep testing your boundaries. Even though you've broken the back of your phobia, you've still got to keep putting yourself into situations which might make you feel uncomfortable.

So how do you make sure you do that? The best way is to add it to your diary, so for the first three months you have an appointment once a week to seek out a challenge. If you plan what you're going to do before you do it, you'll have a commitment to see it through and it will be harder for you to duck out. Someone who had a fear of birds, for instance, could go to the park regularly to feed the ducks, or walk through the busiest part of town where the pigeons hang out.

Just give yourself small, regular everyday tasks which keep you in practice. This will also go a long way towards 'proving' to yourself you don't have a phobia any more, which is one of the worries you've probably got.

Since I got over my fear of birds I've made a conscious effort to put myself in situations where birds are. I've taken my daughter to the local farm which has ostriches, turkeys and geese (to name a few) for the first time; I've also taken her to feed tropical birds at the zoo as well as taking her to the duck pond. I honestly didn't realise how much my phobia was affecting my life until it was gone. I can walk through town now with a clear head, thinking normal things like what to cook for dinner, instead of worrying about where the next pigeon is going to be. I think the biggest different I've noticed in terms of relationships has been with friends. Although there's the odd joke here and there, the majority seem to have a genuine respect for me for taking on my fears. It's crazy how many people have since admitted their own fears to me, and I find myself trying to help them and pass on Richard's pearls of wisdom. It just feels like the bird phobia was a ball and chain around my ankle. I'd learned to live with it, but now it's gone I realise how much it was holding me back. I truly feel able to take anything on.

Guy, who had a bird phobia before he worked with me on Extreme Phobias, Extreme Cures

On a weekly basis I attend my local pet store, where they are teaching me more in depth about handling spiders and cleaning out their habitats. In the near future I'll be looking to own my own tarantula.

Daniel, who had a spider phobia before he worked with me on Extreme Phobias, Extreme Cures

Living in the real world

Having a phobia can be a bit like carrying around a comfort blanket. Being terrified of something means you don't have to do it, which also means there are other things (and people) you can avoid as well. Although you didn't start off with this intention, it will slowly have become a reality for you.

So how do you work through this? There are three main areas to focus on here:

- Developing assertiveness
- Learning to live with uncertainty
- Avoiding 'black-and-white' thinking

Developing assertiveness

Up until now you may have avoided people who didn't have the same degree of consideration for your needs as those close to you, as it was a way of managing the embarrassment around your phobia. You could always rely on your partner or best friend to 'fill in the gaps' so you didn't have to do what you were scared of.

But now you need to deal with all sorts of people, not just your trusted circle. Post-phobia life is not about you living on your own terms, but about marrying what you need with what other people want as well.

One of the things I find when I help people overcome their phobias, is they avoid talking about their fears and this can lead to even more anxiety. It can be very helpful to express yourself more – so rather than keeping it in when you feel bothered by something, have a conversation about it instead.

This can be difficult if you're not sure how to be assertive in a balanced way, or to negotiate for what you need without being aggressive. You may have got used to living in a world in which you had a lot of control, as that's the effect your phobia had on those around you. Especially if it was a social phobia or agoraphobia, it can be hard to adjust to a 'real world' where not everything goes your way.

If you think you'll find it hard to be assertive in a way that works (rather than causing an argument or leading to you backing down), there's an 'Assertiveness That Works' page in the Support Materials at the end of this book. Take a look.

Learning to live with uncertainty

Another thing you may find hard to comes to terms with is learning to live with a degree of uncertainty. When you had a phobia, your fears about being out of control were channelled into avoiding a panic attack. But now you don't have that any more, you'll need to create ways of loosening your control over everyday events.

For some people this can be harder than others, so you may find an exercise called the *3 Cs* useful here. It's based on Control, Choice and Consequences. The idea is that in any situation we have a certain degree of control, and it's the process of recognising and accepting the level of control we have that sets us free.

I'll give you an example. You're waiting for a train to an important meeting. An announcement comes over the tannoy telling you the train is delayed. You have no control over this, but you *do* have control over how you react. You can either accept the situation (get a coffee and relax), or mutter under your breath, stomp up and down the platform and get frustrated. Either way the train is late, it's your choice of reaction that makes the difference.

So in this scenario:

- **Control:** the train being late is out of your control
- **Choice:** you can choose to accept it or get annoyed
- **Consequences:** accepting it will lead to calm and peace, whereas getting annoyed will make you feel anxious and stressed

The Support Materials section at the end of this book gives you a nice breakdown of how this works in any situation.

'Black-and-white' thinking

If there's one thing that unites many people with phobias, it's the habit of thinking in a 'black-and-white' or 'all-or-nothing' kind of way. This is because when you had a phobia, your protective instincts told you not to go anywhere near the source of your fear; there was little room for compromise.

The problem is, this way of behaving cuts you off from new experiences. If you're not open-minded to change, you're missing out on all sorts of new and exciting things coming into your life.

I often find when people come off the back of a phobia they have quite a defensive viewpoint. It's fear that causes this, because they're often looking for the worst-case scenario. A good antidote is for you to think, 'What's the best that could happen?' rather than 'What's the worst that could happen?' Or to reflect on your positives at the end of every day: things you've enjoyed, learned and achieved. Even if you've had a really bad day you've discovered what you'll do differently next time, and you're re-educating your brain to approach your life with a more positive and joyful mind-set.

You've probably been thinking in black and white for a long time, so it can be hard to catch yourself doing it. Why not ask your buddy to gently point out when they see you behaving in an 'all-or-nothing' kind of way, so you can work out a middle ground?

It's a springboard

Beating your phobia is only the start of good things happening to you. The techniques and strategies you've used will also help you deal with additional problems that life may throw up. In other words, you've learned to be your own therapist.

So whether you feel nervous about going for a new job, or to a party where you don't know anyone, you've discovered some brilliant coping methods that are equally applicable to any new and daunting situation. One of the best bits of feedback I get from my clients who've overcome their phobias is that it's taught them the skills and confidence to take on a lot more challenges in their lives.

You've got a new momentum now. So ask yourself, what else could you be doing? Is there something you've always dreamed of taking on? What about moving to a new area, travelling to a particular country, or joining that online dating site your friend is always going on about? You can tackle anything now!

One of the nicest things to do is to help other people with similar problems to the ones you've had. Not only does this inspire them, but it also cements your own knowledge and understanding – you're proving to yourself how much you've learned and achieved. By moving from victim to teacher, you'll be boosting your own self esteem.

Another positive that's come out of beating my bird phobia, is that an old friend of mine got in touch to see if I could give her some advice on helping her granddaughter overcome her phobia of sheep (they live on a farm, so you can see how hard this is). I have offered to talk to the young girl and her mum, and also encourage the family to watch the series.

Ann-Marie, who had a bird phobia before she worked with me on Extreme Phobias, Extreme Cures

You've come such a long way, and as your life unfolds you'll embrace many new and exciting people, places and things. This is only the beginning of your phobia-free life.

Would you like more inspiration? Flip to Chapter 7 for some wonderful success stories.

What we learned in Chapter 6

- If you've used this book to overcome your phobia – or even if you're still getting there – well done. Reward yourself.

- It can take a while to get used to not having a phobia. You may not trust yourself to keep progressing, or be sure your phobia's really gone.

- Losing one fear can mean having to confront another. There will be lots of things you will now need to deal with, which you opted out of before.

- To cope with this, take things slowly and don't feel you have to go it alone.

- Make regular appointments to do challenging things, so you don't regress.

- Learning how to deal with difficult situations and people, and with uncertainty and lack of control, are part of living your life without your phobia.

- Black-and-white thinking is common in people with phobias. Your task is now to move away from 'all-or-nothing' scenarios and to learn to accept compromise.

- This is only the beginning. The skills and techniques you've learned by overcoming your phobia can now be put to use in many new challenges and experiences in your life.

Chapter 7

Success Stories

There's nothing like hearing how other people have succeeded to get your motivational juices flowing. I've been sharing snippets of successes with you so far, but now I want you to get a real taste of how beating their phobias has changed the lives of some of the people I've worked with.

These particular stories are from the TV show I worked on called *Extreme Phobias, Extreme Cures*; so when you see them referring to that, you'll understand what it means. The people took part in group exposure therapy so it was a slightly different process to what you've read about in this book, but the transformation they experienced is the same.

Below you'll see several stories – in their own words – of ordinary people, just like you, who never thought they'd stop being afraid of something. But they did, and you can too. Please enjoy reading these stories; they could be yours one day.

Neil's story

I'm Neil, I'm 60 years old and I'm an actor and embroiderer (I used to be a solicitor and musician). I live with my partner and our three children, aged 24, 20 and 16.

My water phobia made me afraid to put my head under water, or even under the running shower. I was fine with boats and being out in the rain (I love a good storm), although I know a lot of people with a water phobia are not.

This meant I avoided baths and was very tentative in the shower, only standing with my back to the water and being very careful not to get it on my face. Swimming pools were a no-no; I could swim, but would only do breast stroke so as to keep my head out of the water.

The hardest thing about having the phobia was sitting at the side of the pool as my kids played with their friends. As they were growing up, becoming confident swimmers and enjoying their summers around the pool in Spain, my phobia was getting worse. They knew I didn't like the pool, but they really had no idea I was becoming increasingly terrified at the thought of going in there.

I honestly have no idea why this phobia occurred. As a child I was fine with water and had no reason to believe it would ever be a problem. But over the last few years it had sneaked up on me, and I began to realise I had a real issue with it.

Every other problem I've encountered in my life, I've managed to resolve quite quickly, but this one was a real monkey on my back. And it wasn't as if I could talk to my family about it, as they had no idea how deep the phobia ran within me. A couple of years ago, one of my sons wanted to learn how to scuba dive, so I took him to the local club where he took to it easily and enjoyed it immensely. He tried to get me to give it a go, so one evening (when he wasn't there) I went to a trial session. When I tried to put my head under I became a flailing idiot, and no matter what the instructors said or did, I just panicked more until they finally gave in. I was their first 'failure'.

It wasn't until I came across a TV show looking for people with phobias that I did anything about it. After all, it wasn't restricting my life and I'd developed many strategies for coping with it. But something in the advert for people for the show struck a chord, and I applied.

Before I knew it, I was meeting nine other people with the same phobia as me. We didn't know it at the time, but the next three days would change our lives for ever. We went from gently getting into the shallow end of the pool wearing a life jacket, to jumping from six feet high into 12 feet of water with an extreme wave machine and storm conditions.

Amazingly, after our day in the water tank I went for a shower without thinking. I just headed straight in head first rather than reversing in, and avoiding getting the water on my face. I don't avoid the bath any more either.

A couple of weeks ago we went on a family holiday to Spain. As usual, I laid on a sunbed while everyone else was in the water. I wanted to cool down, so I thought about the day in the water tank and made a decision. I walked calmly over to the pool and dived, yes dived, in! There was no panic before, during or after. The only ill effect was the rather painful red chest and stomach caused by the belly flop; it turns out it's not as easy as Tom Daley makes it look!

Kelly's story

My name is Kelly. I'm 31, and before having children I worked in the legal profession. I'm currently taking a break from work until my youngest child starts school.

I'm married to Oliver, and we live with our daughter and son, aged four and two.

My phobia was of birds, and I've had it since early childhood. I believe it was caused by a bird flying out of a bush and flapping close to my face when I was a toddler strapped to the top of my brother's pram.

I always found it very embarrassing having a phobia, and tried not to say too much to people about it. I avoided as many situations as possible where there were birds. I planned my life around it.

My family were sympathetic, but it made life difficult for them. Other people often found it really funny; they laughed at me a lot.

The main obstacle to overcoming my phobia was that I didn't actually believe I could do it. I'd had it for so long; it was so severe; and I'd tried so many things unsuccessfully in the past. I would start enthusiastically, and then get put off when anything seemed too difficult. I'm inclined to panic!

I worked hard with graded exposure which I found really helpful. Gradually building up made it more manageable on my own.

I don't consider myself completely cured yet, but I would now describe myself as not being keen on birds rather than having a phobia. My life is so much easier, as I am confident that I can deal with bird situations. I can do so much that I couldn't do before, and am generally more relaxed. My life has completely changed, and I am so much happier.

If you have a phobia, keep trying! Everything you do is something towards the end goal of not being held back by fear. Believe in yourself. I went from crying when a sparrow landed ten feet away, to holding a dove in my hands, working on a turkey farm and having an owl land on my head. If I can do it, anyone can.

Richard said to me something which has stayed with me, and that I use almost every day. He told me to think of my fear as an old friend that I've outgrown, who's trying to hold me back. When I hear that voice telling me I can't do something, I remember his words and ignore that old friend. I hope one day that friend will be left behind for ever. I'm working on it.

There is a life without fear waiting for you – just go and get it for yourself!

William's story

My name's William, I'm 20 years old and I'm currently working in retail as a gap job. My phobia was the sea and deep water, but now I'm waiting for my results after applying for a job on a cruise ship. Unbelievable, isn't it?

My phobia started when I was very young. I was on a beach holiday with my parents; my dad and brother were swimming at sea, and a strong undercurrent took my brother by surprise. My dad swam off to save him and I was left alone since I was the older child. I wasn't a strong swimmer, and I was terrified. I haven't been on a beach holiday since!

I never visited the seaside and avoided all water sports. I think the main part of my phobia was fear of the unknown, and the bottomless depths of the water. I once went on a small boat ride to watch seals off-shore, and spent the entire time keeping track of how far I had to swim in case the boat capsized.

I found it difficult to share my phobia with others – even my family – and made up excuses when invited on holiday. I suspected people would make fun of me, or would think I was attention seeking, which was really upsetting.

It was easy to avoid the fear rather than face it, but the key to success in overcoming my phobia was meeting others in the same boat (pardon the pun). Working as a team and encouraging the others really helped me to encourage myself. I had to remind myself it was all psychological and was only going to affect me as long as I let it.

Since the show I've been so much more confident as a person – not just in water, but around friends, girls and so on. I feel like a new person. As well as applying for a cruise ship job, I've booked two holidays this year to Florida and Spain. I can't believe I'm looking forward to the beach!

A couple of months ago, I would have died at the thought of even thinking that. So the moral of the story is, that I wanted to have fun more than I wanted to let my phobia take control.

Peter's story

I'm Peter, aged 50, single and an insurance company manager. My phobia was heights. It probably started when I visited Blackpool with my family aged eight, and froze at the top of Blackpool Tower. I clearly remember standing at the top, deliberately staying away from the ledge and avoiding looking down below. I felt such relief when we arrived down on the ground.

My initial beliefs were that the phobia was frustrating, as others didn't appear to be affected. I believed it seemed ridiculous and that I shouldn't be feeling this way. I tended to avoid situations such as tourist attractions, which was annoying especially with friends who I was travelling with. They felt it was illogical, as it was safe and nothing was going to happen.

There were various setbacks over the years, particularly when I travelled to Paris with a girlfriend and was unable to go near the Eiffel Tower; just looking at the building made me feel really sick. I was also terrified of flying, which caused a number of problems. When I finally managed to get on a plane, I was a nervous wreck and had to be calmed down by the airline staff.

I took part in group exposure therapy, which involved various challenges to do with heights. I felt very uncomfortable and frightened, but the exercises proved to be beneficial, especially with the expert guidance nearby and encouragement from the group. I felt ecstatic as I conquered each challenge, although I was disappointed when I didn't finish the final one. I did, however, learn that I need to be kind to myself, and also developed numerous tools and techniques which helped me focus on something else as a distraction from my fear.

Since then, I've noticed an increased confidence in myself in terms of taking on other challenges. My relationships have improved significantly, and my friends and colleagues have noticed an improvement in my confidence and drive to succeed. I'm an emergency first aider at work, and recently won an award as there was a major incident and I was praised for keeping calm under extreme pressure. I used the techniques I learned on the show to keep both myself and the patient level headed and calm.

Joshua's story

My name is Joshua, I'm 21, a psychology student, and I live with my mum, her boyfriend and my younger brother. I've been in a civil partnership for six months now. I had a water phobia and I believe it originated with falling off an inflatable into deep pool water when I was young. Also, my nan is a water phobic so that may have contributed.

I wasn't too bothered by it for a while. I knew most of my family would think I was dramatic if I made too much fuss, so I just sort of avoided water. Eventually it became noticeable at the beach, and my family knew. As I got older I wanted to overcome it, as it was getting in the way of bonding opportunities such as taking my little brother swimming. I decided I would lose out on family time if I didn't gather the courage to get over my phobia.

While taking part in the show, I found it fascinating as a psychology student how paranoid we all got so quickly, and just how much we catastrophised everything. The hardest thing was getting in a water tank. I felt my throat get a lump in it and tears start to form in my eyes. I got sweaty palms and a faster heart rate, but I didn't want to embarrass myself, so I held it together. The few seconds under the water really panicked me, but as soon as my head was on the surface again I felt so proud and really relieved. After the first jump it all became quite fun; I was shocked to find myself laughing after a while, and just enjoying the experience.

Since then, I can finally join my family on the beach and go swimming with them when we are on holiday. I've even gone so far as to swim in the sea with my mum, which is something I considered to be my absolute worst nightmare before. It's brought my family and I much closer together, because I don't spoil days out by refusing to participate in activities. It makes our holidays complete.

The biggest change has been between me and my little brother. He was always begging me to swim with him and I always refused because of my phobia. Since the show, I've been playing ball in the pool with him; he didn't understand my phobia and I think he just thought I didn't want to play with him which hurt his feelings, so now he's overjoyed that I can join in.

Daniel's story

Ever since I can remember I've had this severe phobia of spiders. Every time I came across one of those devilish creatures my whole body would shake with fright, I would see or feel nothing but pure fear, and I would sweat profusely. All over something so small. My main concern was the thought of being bitten and the spider causing serious harm, or even death. I was constantly moving home if I had seen a spider where I lived; in the space of five years I averaged around 27 homes. I even injured myself while trying to escape the presence of spiders.

After suffering for so long, I thought I would be stuck with this crippling nightmare for ever. But going on the TV show was the best decision of my life. Although I was thrown in at the deep end and didn't know how to react, it was surprisingly soothing knowing there were others around for support. With each day that went by, this fear seemed to just melt away. It was strange that a phobia which had taken over my life for so long, was vanishing over the space of 72 hours.

That's it, I've done it, I've managed to handle a tarantula and even been able to explain to a group of spectators that handling spiders has to be done with a lot of care. No longer am I running away, no longer are spiders my biggest fear, and no longer are they taking over my life.

Now, my life is amazing. No more moving house for me when I spot a spider. My partner is really impressed with the progress I've made more recently, too. On a weekly basis I attend my local pet store, where they are teaching me more in depth about handling spiders and cleaning out their habitats. In the near future I'll be looking to own my own tarantula.

I think the three best words I can use, and which make me feel great when I say them, are: I AM CURED!

Chapter 8

Family and Friends

As someone with a phobia, you will no doubt have leaned on your friends and family to help you cope. Whether it be through emotional support or through practical help with avoiding the source of your fear, they will have been affected by your phobia too.

This chapter is for those people to read. I'd encourage you to show it to them so they can get the support they need as well.

To you, friends and family ...

If your loved one has had a phobia for a long time, and depending on how disabling it's been, you may have got used to being a support system for them. It can become like a co-dependency, where you make changes in your life to keep them in their comfort zone. And you've done it out of love and concern.

In Chapter 2, I talked about the importance of a buddy for someone trying to beat their phobia. And in Chapter 5, the role of the buddy became crystal clear in the exposure ladders. You may or may not have been your phobic's buddy, but even if you weren't, I'm sure you will still have played a big role in managing their fears and in promoting their recovery.

But what happens when that person doesn't have a phobia any more? Of course, it's fantastic to be able to do things you might not have been able to enjoy in the past, such as travelling to new places and taking days out. You might also be enjoying *not* doing things you used to have to do, such as all the shopping and being the only one who could take the kids to the swimming pool.

However, there's no getting away from the fact that it changes the balance in your relationship. When you were helping your loved one with their phobia, your identity was partly that of a carer. So now your support-ive role is no longer there, you might feel a bit lost or even threatened. Their life is starting to blossom, but yours hasn't been through such a positive transform-ation, and this might not feel so good.

If this happens (and it might not, it depends on your own situation), it's important to talk about how you feel. Don't bottle it up – share your thoughts so you can both deal with this together. You may have got used to avoiding talking about the phobia for fear of provoking anxiety and upset, but it doesn't have to be this way any more.

What would you love to do?

You still have a support role to fill for a while. Encouraging your partner to keep challenging themselves each week is really important (see Chapter 6 for more detail on that).

But now you don't have to help your partner in the same way as you used to, is there anything you've been putting on hold you could revisit? Is it going to the gym, picking up a hobby, or getting back on top with your career? If you're honest with yourself, were there challenges you didn't face up to before because of your partner's phobia? Did you even use it as an excuse? Now's the time to take a look at your life and work out what you need in order to be fulfilled.

There are also experiences you can have as a couple that will help you to grow together. Now you're a phobia-free unit, you can find all sorts of new ways to connect!

Afternote

If I've helped even one person to overcome their phobia with this book, I'll have achieved my objective. Of course, I'm hoping there are many more phobia sufferers who've found inspiration in these pages, and that one of them is you.

But this is more than just a book, it's a whole host of online resources which add to this book's effectiveness. Please head on over to http://richardreidmedia.com/thehub/cure_your_phobia, where you can download various resources.

I'm looking forward to welcoming you.

Richard Reid

Support Materials

Assertiveness that Works

Assertiveness involves:

- Respect for self and others
- Taking responsibility for thoughts, feelings and actions
- Recognising and making choices
- Pay-offs: results, opportunities, good relationships

Three Step Model

1. Listen and acknowledge: '*I understand you want to go out with your friends now...*'
2. Say what you think: '*However, it's too late for tonight as you have school tomorrow*'

3. Say what you want to happen and talk about benefits: '*We can sort something out for tomorrow night in the morning*'

Managing Instant Reactions

1. Count to 10 in your head
2. Less is more
3. Keep it Short and Simple (K.I.S.S.)

Assertive Body Language

- Breathing (slow and deep)
- Eye contact
- Facial expression
- Gestures
- Personal space
- Posture
- Voice and speech pattern

Control, Choice, Consequence (3 C's)

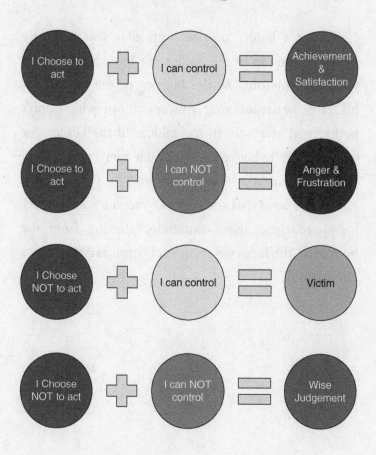

Exposure Ladder

Construct a ladder of situations that you currently avoid. At the top of the ladder put those which make you most anxious. At the bottom of the ladder put places or situations that you avoid, but which don't bother you as much. In the middle of the ladder put ones that are 'in between'. Give each item a rating from 0-100% according to how anxious you would feel if you had to be in that situation. Overcome your anxiety by approaching these situations, starting from the bottom of the ladder. Repeat each stage as many times as necessary.

Activity	Anxiety Rating 0–100%	Hour 1–24	Insights & Learning

Useful Resources

http://www.phobics-society.org.uk/

https://www.anxietyuk.org.uk/

http://phobialist.com/

http://www.nhs.uk/Conditions/Phobias/Pages/Introduction.aspx

http://www.mind.org.uk/information-support/types-of-mental-health-problems/phobias/

http://www.moodjuice.scot.nhs.uk/phobias.asp

Index

Page references in *italics* indicate illustrations.

418117
BETTWS